CW00410759

ENDORSEMENTS

Finally, a message about the power of our words and the necessity of speaking life, which is convicting, balanced, transparent, and highly practical. Katherine has presented an essential Christian theology here, wrapped in a revelation of God's abundant loving nature, as well as our new nature in Christ. If diligently applied, these lessons, illustrated from Katherine's own life stories and history with God, will impact our everyday lives in momentous ways.

Often, our confessions and declarations can carry a subconscious motive of twisting God's arm, as we hope to receive from Him what we feel He is reluctant to give us. Katherine fiercely presents the heart of God and His already purchased and provided inheritance for His saints. This book will challenge you to think differently about Father God's will for you, as well as who you are in Christ.

I have been personally challenged by this book and reminded about the power of speaking God's Will over myself, my marriage, my friends, my destiny, and my circumstances. Knowing Katherine closely, I have loved learning from her as she daily practices the principles shared in this book. *Speak Life!*

MARK GREENWOOD
Author of *Awake to Righteousness*
Founder - The Jesus School
Director - The Academy
Pastor - Glory City Church, Brisbane

Psychiatrists tell us that 80% of our self-talk is negative. Since we reap what we sow, just imagine the bad harvest we are getting every day. In *Speak Life*, Katherine Ruonala gives us a masterful review of the need to change and then practical steps on how to change the conversation and then speak life over ourselves, others, and our circumstances. May you be inspired to change the words you sow, and then rejoice over the change in your harvest.

GORDON ROBERTSON
CEO, The Christian Broadcasting Network

When we speak, we can either make a deposit that increases a person's worth or a withdrawal, detracting from their sense of worth. *Speak Life*, by my friend Katherine Ruonala aided by the Holy Spirit, has already given me an upgrade and can do the same for you!

LEIF HETLAND
President, Global Mission Awareness
Author of *Giant Slayers*

I love this book!!!!! Faith will be imparted to you as you read it, and I'm also convinced that you will receive some healthy, holy conviction regarding the words you speak—at least it did this for me. *Speak Life* is a much-needed message today, and I am indeed grateful that Katherine has served us with this wonderful message.

PATRICIA KING
Founder of Patricia King Ministries

God's words will create God's world! When you learn how to speak what God is saying, you will practically and measurably begin to see "Thy Kingdom come" become a reality in your everyday life.

We are created to be images of God in the Earth. One of the ways we do this is by speaking like Him. In *Speak Life*, my friend, Pastor Katherine Ruonala, gives you prophetic strategies to bring your words into agreement with what God says about your circumstances.

This book is timely and refreshing. What I appreciate about Katherine's perspective is that it is not some kind of stale formula; we speak words of life because we live in a place of intimacy with the Author of Life. Katherine models this. She lives and conducts her ministry with an ear ever pressed upon the heart of Heaven.

Speak Life will practically show you how to access the power, solutions, and miracles that come from the heavenly realm and prophesy them into your life by boldly declaring His words. As you put these life-giving principles into practice, I believe your words will become a resting place for the Holy Spirit, so that like Jesus, you can make decrees that release the Spirit of God and the life of Heaven!

LARRY SPARKS, MDIV.
Publisher, Destiny Image
www.larrysparksministries.com
Author of *Breakthrough Faith*, co-author of *The Fire That Never Sleeps,* and co-author of *Arise* with Patricia King

As I read through the pages of this manuscript, it quickly became apparent that this message, which is so beautifully written, is truly life changing. The tools that Katherine has scribed in each chapter hold a divine key to true impartation, discipleship, and transformation. *Speak Life* will empower you to identify and overcome thoughts, mind-sets, words, and actions that have held back the breakthrough and victory that our heavenly Father has ordained. As the promises of the message are applied, you will enter into a spiritual life secure in your kingdom identity and the obtain faith for a life of joy and triumph. Friend, now is your time to arise and shine in the promises of your Kingdom inheritance.

REBECCA GREENWOOD
President
Christian Harvest International
Strategic Prayer Apostolic Network
Author of *Defeating Strongholds of the Mind, Let Our Children Go, Your Kingdom Come, Glory Warfare*

Katherine Ruonala's book *Speak Life* is a deep treasury of revelation, wisdom, and practical keys to aligning ourselves with the Word of God through our decrees and seeing the power of God's Word manifest in our lives. This book carries a beautiful impartation of awakening to new realms of faith in the nature of God and the power of His Word and Truth. *Speak Life* is a weapon given to you to refer back to, time and time again, to assist you in your life as you "fight the good fight of faith." From the lists of powerful decrees, to Katherine's personal stories and testimonies, I know this book will increase your hunger to know Jesus and His Word and to walk in greater realms of victory, faith, and joy that have been given to you in Christ. Breakthrough awaits you!

LANA VAWSER
Founder of Lana Vawser Ministries,
Author of *The Prophetic Voice of God*
lanavawser.com

"You can have what you say." Right from the outset, Katherine's book *Speak Life* will draw you into a world of revelation that will have you picking up this book more than once. It is full of life-giving, practical applications of truths that mean people find keys to success, happiness, joy, and peace. Based on the theology that we are created in God's image, this book paints a new picture of the way we can speak and the way we think. It activates spiritual understanding in the life of the believer and draws us further into a dynamic and exciting adventure of faith. The teachings in this book will propel you forward in your God-given destiny and will give you some of the main tools needed to be all that God has called you to be. What a statement "We are called to be overcomers who create whatever is good"! Amen to that! But does it work? Is it true? I have the great joy of working with Katherine and her husband, Tom, on a daily basis in the senior leadership of Glory City Church, the TV ministry, and the ever-expanding outreaches and stadium events. We often minister together and do conferences together. In all of that busy ministry interaction, there are the good times, the victory times, and also the challenges and disappointments. Over the years of working with Katherine, I have seen her consistently put this book into practice. I have been inspired, as time and time again, day after day, I have seen her apply this as a way of life. I can testify that this book has risen from a wellspring of tested and proven life experience. I have seen Katherine change the atmosphere in some tough situations, and it is so glorious to see. For example, I remember the day we were on the way to negotiate a deal with one of the biggest Christian TV networks in the US. We had some TV executives and agents in the car. We started to play "Katherine's game." It's a game where we call that which is not as if it were. We started declaring statements like "My children are married to God-fearing spouses," "This TV channel loves me and wants me on their program," "They love the ministry so much they want to give us the best rate possible"... and so the game went on. You should have seen the raised eyebrows on our accompanying friends as Katherine, Tom, and I actively got into Katherine's game; we were making bold declarations and calling outlandish favour forward. Well... history repeats itself. Days later, raised eyebrows were complemented by dropped jaws and mouths open wide as our unusual but enjoyable way of doing business came true, and what we had spoken in faith materialised into present reality. Read this book and you will receive great revelation. Apply this book, and it will change your life.

PASTOR DANIEL ZELLI
Senior Apostolic Leader Glory City Network of Churches
CEO and Co-Leader World Hope Network

SPEAK
LIFE

CREATING YOUR WORLD WITH YOUR WORDS

KATHERINE RUONALA

SPEAK LIFE
CREATING YOUR WORLD WITH YOUR WORDS
Katherine Ruonala

Copyright © Katherine Ruonala 2019. All rights reserved. Except for brief quotations for review purposes, no part of this book may be reproduced in any form without prior written permission from the author.

Unless otherwise noted, scripture quotations are taken from the New King James Version®. Copyright © 1982 by Thomas Nelson. Used by permission. All rights reserved.

Scripture quotations marked TPT are from The Passion Translation®. Copyright © 2017, 2018 by Passion & Fire Ministries, Inc. Used by permission. All rights reserved. ThePassionTranslation.com.

Scripture quotations marked (NIV) are taken from the Holy Bible, New International Version®, NIV®. Copyright © 1973, 1978, 1984, 2011 by Biblica, Inc.™ Used by permission of Zondervan. All rights reserved worldwide. www.zondervan.com The "NIV" and "New International Version" are trademarks registered in the United States Patent and Trademark Office by Biblica, Inc.™

Scripture quotations from The Authorized (King James) Version. Rights in the Authorized Version in the United Kingdom are vested in the Crown. Reproduced by permission of the Crown's patentee, Cambridge University Press.

Cover Design and Interior Layout | Yvonne Parks | PearCreative.ca

ISBN: (Print) 978-0-6485568-0-0
ISBN: (eBook) 978-0-6485568-1-7

ACKNOWLEDGMENTS

Tom Ruonala, thank you for all your help and patience with helping to put this book together. I love you!

My friend Sarah Cheesman, what a delight it is to have your encouragement and help. I so appreciate your commitment to speaking life and playing my game with me over the years, your zeal and powerful encouragements, your skills in editing, and your constant faith and hope for the future.

My mum, Roslyn Mills, thank you once again for your editing assistance and encouragement.

Dom Arama, thank you for your encouragement and help in proofreading.

Wendy Joyce, you are amazing! Thank you for your wonderful help, keen eye, and great encouragement. What a blessing you are.

TABLE OF CONTENTS

FOREWORD

JAMES W. GOLL

Over the years I learned a principle out of Ezekiel 37. The prophet was taken into a valley of dry bones where everything was fragmented, out of joint, and where there weren't any signs of life. Ezekiel was being guided by the Holy Spirit in a personal manner and was being taught valuable lessons for life and ministry. He was instructed to "prophesy life" over Israel's destiny when it was in disarray and brokenness.

To prophesy life also means to *declare* or to *speak* with Inspiration. Thus, the prophet of God was called to rise above the temporary problematic circumstances that existed and was given Heaven's remedy for the earthly dilemma. This is one of God's solutions for man's problems. Yes, it is called speaking life!

A great company of change makers has walked in this supernatural dimension for many, many years. Abraham did it. Ezekiel declared it. Joseph walked in it. Esther modeled it. Mary exemplified it. Jesus emphasized it. And my friend, Katherine Ruonala, is in good company as she teaches us to do it as well. Most of us are aware that our very words carry the power of death and life. Our words not only impact us, but they can have a profound effect on the people and events around us. I teach people to look for the redemptive path. Call upon the Lord! Come up higher and get God's perspective on things. Graft His thoughts into your mind and heart and lean into the Holy Spirit to conceive His wisdom ways. Then speak forth life from this alternative, opposite spirit waging effective spiritual warfare through the power of your speech. Your words become impregnated with God's Word, and His Word never returns void!

Let's stop tearing ourselves, family members, others, leaders of various spheres, our cities, and nations down. Stop it! Let's be creators of atmospheres and realms. Let's be partners with the Holy Spirit. Let's speak life over every cultural sphere in Jesus' name!

In Katherine's wonderful book, *Speak Life*, she teaches us how "You Can Have What You Say," "Aligning Your Words with God's," and how to be a believer "Walking in Triumph." Come up higher and speak life. Jesus did and He is calling you to join Him in this exciting lifestyle.

With Expectation,

JAMES W. GOLL

God Encounters Ministries

1

YOU CAN HAVE
WHAT YOU SAY

UNDERSTANDING THE
POWER OF WORDS

"Poor Tom…" In my mind, it was a trivial comment about my husband for what he had to put up with on a ministry trip to South Korea. We had spent a few days with several amazing Christian leaders from around the world, and God was doing some wonderful things in our meetings. I so enjoyed seeing Him heal, deliver, and save people who were hungry for Him, and I loved spending time with other ministry leaders. But when I made my off-the-cuff comment, pitying Tom for some inconvenience, one of those leaders interrupted me. "Why would you say that about your husband? Why would you call him 'poor'?"

I was suddenly hit with conviction. I knew better. I preach about the power of words all the time. I understand that I'm created in the image of God, who created the world with His words. I know what negative words can do, and it bothers me when I hear people use them carelessly. So when I let this comment slip, I was actually grateful for the friendly reminder. I would never want to speak something harmful over my husband.

I realize that may sound overly religious and legalistic to some people. Most of us are used to speaking casually, freely using figures of speech and common idioms to express our thoughts. We say things like "poor so-and-so" or "what a shame" or "that makes me sick" without actually intending anything negative. These words are just expressions, aren't they? At least that's how we mean them. But if I actually believe what I've been teaching, that we are children of a God who created the world with His words, who calls things that are not as though they are, who speaks life and light into existence, then I need to speak as though my words really matter. They accomplish things. As someone made in the image of God, my words have creative power. It's a power I have to use responsibly.

That's true for all of us. Believers in Jesus have the power to speak and create the world around us with our words. Why? Because it's no longer we who live but Christ who lives in us (Galatians 2:20). We have been given an amazing gift. Since much will be required from those who have been given much (Luke 12:48), we have a great responsibility. We have to be diligent and disciplined to use our words the way God meant for us to use them, whether we have our minds in gear or not, whether we are speaking in public or just talking casually. Words matter even when we aren't conscious that they do.

Our words play a significant part in creating the world around us, affecting the lives that intersect with ours and circumstances we face. In the week before Jesus' crucifixion, He and His disciples were leaving Jerusalem to stay in nearby Bethany and Jesus was hungry. He saw a fig tree, but it was bearing no fruit, so He condemned it. When they passed by it again later, the disciples noticed that it had withered away. Jesus took the opportunity to teach them a profound spiritual lesson:

> *"Have faith in God. For assuredly, I say to you, whoever says to this mountain, 'Be removed and be cast into the sea,' and does not doubt in his heart, but believes that those things he says will be done, he will have whatever he says. Therefore I say to you, whatever things you ask when you pray, believe that you receive them, and you will have them." (Mark 11:22–24)*

As someone who has spiritually grown up with an awareness of prophetic ministry, I'm very conscious of the power of our words. That's why I'm a little surprised when I slip back into old habits, as I did in South Korea. I have known for a long time why it's important to be very deliberate about what I'm saying. Since I have stopped using the words "Poor Tom," my husband has received several unexpected financial blessings. Just a coincidence? Over the years, through study of the Bible and lots of experience, I've become convinced of a very profound, life-changing truth: I can have what I say.

When I was in South Korea, I heard Yonggi Cho give a testimony about the power of words to heal. In fact, he has personally experienced healing recently. He recalled standing in front of his board, shaking badly from Parkinson's disease, and telling them how embarrassed he was to be seen in that condition. He declared to his international board that the next time they saw him, he would no longer be shaking. The following year, his words had come to pass; he stood and spoke without a tremble. He had combined his faith in God's will to heal and the power of his words to receive healing from God.

Dr. Cho also told a testimony of a woman in the late stages of cancer who had come to him for prayer. He prayed for her again and again, and each time he saw her, there was no improvement. So as a last resort, he told her to take some paper and pencils to Prayer Mountain, a facility owned by his church where people can go for a concentrated time of prayer, and write 10,000 times, "By His stripes I am healed." He told her that every time she wrote that phrase, she should say it out loud. And every time she said it out loud, she should see the prayer answered with her sanctified imagination. So she walked out of his office to do as he had instructed, and he thought to himself, *I think she's going to die.* He admitted not having much faith in his own prescription. She did what he said, and three days later she came back completely healed. The power of her words paired with her vision had prompted a miraculous change in her body.

That's one example of how our words can shape the reality around us. The Bible teaches in many places that we can have what we say. In the following pages, we will explore how Jesus taught His disciples to speak to mountains in order to move them and demonstrated how to calm a storm with words. We will look at several verses from the book of Proverbs that tell us about the fruit of our mouths and how the power of life and death is in our tongues. Combining a faith-filled confession with a Holy-Spirit-empowered vision of answered prayer has become a key part of my life. I could tell testimony after testimony from my life and the lives of others, who have put these truths into practice, to see relationships and circumstances changed through the power of the tongue. When our vision and our words line up with what God is saying, things happen. It's so powerful!

SPEAKING LIFE

Most of us are aware that our words can have a profound effect on the people around us. Spiritual principles aside, the psychological impact of positive and negative comments is not difficult to see. But the Bible takes this even further, teaching us that we have the power to comfort, heal, encourage, and edify on one hand, and on the other hand, to wound and tear people down. A little offhand comment can really hurt someone's heart. I'm aware of that, especially as a leader, a harsh or thoughtless word to someone who looks up to me could cause them great heartache. So I have to be very vigilant about that. I can't afford to have times when my mouth is "off duty." I'm called to love people with the same love God has for me, and He always speaks to me kindly and with great love. I am called to represent Him to people, showing them what God is like, and so I never want to misrepresent His heart of love. For this reason, I thank Him that I'm one of the just who lives by faith, not by feelings, and I thank Him that my identity, anointing, and power are not defined by how well I think I'm doing at any given moment but by the truth that He lives in me. He wants all of us to be fully aware and fully awake, never letting ourselves slip into harmful, critical destructive speech that can tear others down.

As a person filled with Christ, I have the opportunity every day in every relationship to speak wonderful words of life. You do too. We can speak life and truth over ourselves, over our spouses and families, over our churches, over our workplaces, over our communities and governments, and so much more. I've come to take great delight in saying kind words to shopkeepers and restaurant servers and others I come into contact with during the day. "You have lovely eyes," I said to one shop assistant recently, and she was taken aback, obviously unaccustomed to kind words from a stranger. She wanted to know why I would say that, and when I responded, "because it's true," the smile on her face was priceless. Proverbs tells us that an *"anxious heart weighs a man down, but a kind word cheers him up" (Proverbs 12:25, NIV).* Little things have a lot of power to help people experience the love of God. Even when we don't have the opportunity to mention God or explain how someone can come into a relationship with Him, we can demonstrate His heart. We have a tremendous opportunity to express who He is. God wants us to get our hearts in order, fully immersed in His love and mercy, fully aware of His blessings and promises, fully conscious of who we are in Him, because out of the abundance of the heart, the mouth speaks.

I find myself talking to Him often about this. "Okay, Lord, I've got a bit of a negative attitude today. I'm feeling a bit distressed about this. That person really seems to be intent on being difficult. What are Your thoughts about the situation?" And He is so faithful and kind to reveal them. When I get a picture of how much He loves someone, I can align my thoughts and emotions with His and begin to love in the same way. I'm called to take captive every thought that exalts itself against His thoughts, so I do what I can to make that shift, and I ask for His help. "Lord, help me see and experience what it looks like to love them like You do. How does that really feel? What is on Your heart for them? How do You want to respond in this situation?" Once I have heard from Him, I'm able to begin speaking words of grace, prophesying truth, and treating people the way He has treated me.

I have the opportunity every day
in every relationship to speak
wonderful words of life.

This is how we come into agreement with the thoughts and conversations of heaven, the Will of God as it is being expressed among the Father, Son, and Holy Spirit, and bring it into the earthly environment around us. We take captive every thought that exalts itself against the knowledge of Christ, agreeing with truth not only with our minds but also with our mouths. The issue we face all the time is not just knowing what is right; it's applying what we know.

In his book, *The Way of Life*, Bill Johnson discusses this idea of applied wisdom, specifically in the example of Solomon. The Bible says King Solomon was the wisest man to have ever lived. He asked for wisdom, and God gave him that and much, much more. People came from great distances just to hear his wisdom and to marvel at all the wealth and splendor that came from it. Solomon wrote many of the biblical proverbs along with the Song of Songs and Ecclesiastes. We are still able to grow in godly wisdom just by reading and meditating on his profound and inspired words. Sadly, Solomon did not apply all the wisdom he had, and it took Israel years to recover from the results. The kingdom split after his death, his descendants turned to idolatry, and God eventually judged both the northern and southern kingdoms for their rebellion against His truth. We can only imagine what history would have looked like, if Solomon had applied the wisdom he had to every area of his own life. I don't want to make the same kind of mistake, letting spiritual knowledge puff me up without actually working its way into every area of my life. I want to walk in applied wisdom.

One of Solomon's best-known proverbs says, "Trust in the Lord with all your heart and lean not on your own understanding; in all your ways acknowledge Him and He shall direct your paths" (Proverbs 3:5–6). I love to talk about the fellowship of the Holy Spirit, and I want to live in that fellowship to such an extent that I am always aware of His presence. But in thinking about Solomon and his failure to apply wisdom throughout the later years of his life, I began to wonder what it looks like to ask God continually what His wisdom is for a situation and how to apply it. One of the reasons the Holy Spirit was given to us was to remind us of the words of Jesus, to bring to mind the wisdom we've been taught and to show us how it all applies. I want to live from that awareness. I don't just want to know God's wisdom for each situation; I want to speak it. I want my words to bring His wisdom and His light and life into every circumstance I face and every relationship I have.

That's why it's so important to be vigilant about what we say. I believe we are in a season of divine acceleration, of everything, both good and bad. Knowledge is increasing all over the earth, and many in God's kingdom are walking in greater and greater power. At the same time, ignorance about God's ways also seems to be increasing. So as believers, we can't afford to be sowing anything into the world that is not pure, powerful, and true. We have to be intentional about what we do and what we say. We have a tremendous opportunity in these times to walk in the royal authority we've been given, recognizing that our words carry the power of life and death.

We are told not to be conformed to the pattern of the world but to be transformed by the renewing of our minds (Romans 12:2). When we become careless with our words, we are slipping into an old pattern. The new pattern should look like Jesus, and nowhere in His ministry do we see Him being careless about the things He said. In fact, He warned against idle words and taught His disciples to speak purposefully toward other people, toward mountains, toward obstacles, and toward the Father. When our minds are transformed, our words are transformed, and we can then walk in a powerful lifestyle of seeing, declaring, and experiencing answered prayers and promises.

THE RUDDER OF YOUR LIFE

James wrote a lot about the tongue, comparing it to a rudder that steers our lives. That means that we have some control about where we're going to go. Rudders don't rule the ship; they are ruled by the one who is steering the ship. So you can decide which direction your words will lead you. One of the ways I do that is to start my day with some declarations about who I am and what God is doing. I call those things that be not as though they are and remind myself of the truth of my identity in Christ. When I wake up, I like to declare:

- This is the day that the Lord has made and I will rejoice and be glad in it (Psalm 118:24).
- Thank You, Lord. You've laid up good works in advance for me to do today (Ephesians 2:10).
- It's no longer I who live but Christ who lives in me (Galatians 2:20).

- I consider myself dead to sin and alive to God in Christ (Romans 6:11).
- As You are so I am I in this world (John 4:17).
- I am full of power by the Holy Spirit (Micah 3:8).
- I'm strong, I'm alert, I'm healthy, I am the fragrance of Christ (2 Corinthians 2:16).
- My youth is being renewed like the eagles (Psalm 103:5).
- Every day I grow closer to You and I fall more in love with You.
- I am surrounded by Your favor as with a shield (Psalm 5:12).
- I'm the healed of the Lord. Thank You for giving me divine health today. Your life flows through me. By Your stripes I was healed (1 Peter 2:24).
- God is love and because I am as He is in this world, I am loving. Love is patient; therefore, I am patient. I don't try to be patient; it is my nature to be patient. Love is kind, so I am kind. I am kindness personified! Everyone I meet will encounter the kindness of Christ through me today (1 Corinthians 13).
- I reflect You because You are shining Your face on me. I love You, Lord. Thank You that

Your words are in my mouth, that I have Your mind, Your heart, and Your motives. Thank You that You set me free from me and gave me Your nature.

- You have forgiven me.
- By faith I declare that I'm clean, I'm holy, by Your grace I have a clean conscience, and I am as righteous as You are (2 Corinthians 5:21).
- I have Your wisdom and Your mind (1 Corinthians 2:16) and am empowered to make good choices.
- I speak and things happen.

All of those declarations are based on truths and promises from Scripture. They are our inheritance. They are God's will for us. As F. F. Bosworth said, "Faith begins where the will of God is known." We don't have to ask if they are His will when we pray for them and say them; we can go ahead and believe them all and speak them into being. You can probably think of other declarations to add to the list, because Scripture is full of these wonderful blessings and truths. They are the reality we are supposed to walk in. So why not go ahead and declare them? Speak them over your life, even as you begin your day, and you will find yourself walking in greater levels of power.

Not many people know this, but you can have as much as you will see, say, and declare. Your words need to align with the Word of God, of course, but when they do, God wants you to use them to steer the course of your life like a rudder directs a ship. Whether you realize it or not, your words are creating circumstances and experiences around you. You are prophesying even when you don't intend to be prophesying. You have the power to direct your life today, tomorrow, and over the months, years, and decades to come.

IN THE IMAGE OF A CREATOR

In the beginning, God spoke, and the world came into being. He creates with His words. That is clear in Genesis 1, but it also comes up many other times in the Bible. We are told that He upholds all things by the power of His word (Hebrews 1:3); that His voice has power over the forces of nature, thundering from heaven and shaking the wilderness (Psalm 29); that His word will not come back to Him void but will accomplish what it is sent forth to do (Isaiah 55:11); and that He calls things that are not as though they are, and they come to pass (Romans 4:17). This is no surprise for anyone who believes that God is the all-powerful Creator of the world. Of course His words accomplish things; that's His nature.

I remember being in a meeting in Sydney where God was moving in great power, and many people were being miraculously healed in their seats. A couple came up and interrupted the meeting asking for prayer for their son. I could see the desperation and faith in their eyes, and as I went to pray for them, I imagined myself going into their son's hospital room and laying hands on him. I declared him healed in the name of Jesus. I didn't find out the full story until seven years later when the same couple came up to me when I was ministering at a church on the Central Coast in New South Wales. They told me that their son had been diagnosed with end-stage lymphoma and had tumors all through his body; however, the night we prayed, he was instantly healed and had been healthy ever since. God's word, sent forth does not return to Him void but accomplishes what it is sent forth to do!

Have you ever considered that if God can create with His words, and we are made in His image, then perhaps we can create with our words too? While we should never be presumptuous about creating independently of His character and purposes, there is nothing presumptuous about claiming what the Bible says about us. It is not humility to deny the power God wants us to exercise in His name. And Scripture gives us plenty of examples of using our words to create the reality we will experience.

For example, Joshua spoke to the sun and told it to stand still (Joshua 10:12–14), being fully convinced that it was the will of God for Israel to entirely defeat their enemy. Elijah declared that there would be no dew or rain (1 Kings 17:1). Jesus modeled for us how to hear from the Father and then speak what He is saying (John 12:49–50) and to calm storms and wither a fig tree by the power of His words (Mark 4:39–41; 11:20–21). And then, as we have seen, Jesus taught His disciples to speak to mountains and expect them to move (Mark 11:22–24). He gave His followers the keys to the kingdom and the power to bind and loose, all of which involves words of faith and authority. By creating us in His image, the God who created the world with His words gave us the same power.

The Father longs for us to recognize the authority and power we have. This is not something we have to earn, achieve, or even step into. It's something He has already given us. As His body, we operate in the authority of His name. Whatever we ask in His name we will receive. Throughout the Bible, we see that names are very significant to God. The names of God encapsulate who He is—His character, His power, and His personality. The name of Jesus Christ—the Messiah, the Savior, the Son of God, and the Anointed One—is more than just His title; it IS Him. When we use His name, we are not just invoking a formula in obedience to the Lord's command; we are releasing the very tangible reality of who Jesus is.

We can come in intimacy before the Lord and allow Him to hold us, love us, and reassure us that we are not on our own. We are loved and cherished beyond our greatest imagination. In that place, we remember that it is no longer we who live but Christ who lives in us and that we have been crucified with Christ and then resurrected in His power. We have His name, His mind, His Spirit, and breath within us. Anything we do, whether in some act of ministry or just living out our daily lives, we can do in His strength rather than our own. And in His strength, we learn to love as He loves, think as He thinks, and speak as He speaks. We learn to speak life.

God wants us to be very deliberate about using this power. Proverbs tells us:

> *"A man's stomach shall be satisfied from the fruit of his mouth; from the produce of his lips he shall be filled. Death and life are in the power of the tongue and those who love it will eat its fruit." (Proverbs 18:20–21)*

Our words carry power to bring life or death. That's a lot of responsibility, but it's also a wonderful opportunity. What are you going to do with it? I know too many believers who use their words to describe all the bad things that seem to be going on in their lives. They see themselves, other people, and situations in the natural realm and just reaffirm what they see. Anyone can do that; it's easy. But God doesn't ask us to call those things that are as they are. He teaches us to call those things that are not, as though they are. He gives us the opportunity to reenvision and re-create the environment around us according to His will and the desires He has put in our hearts.

I've seen people get old before their time because they hang around people who speak negatively and they start speaking that way themselves. I've heard people in their 40s say things like, "You know how it is with people *our age*. We can't really do those things anymore . . ." In their 40s! Why would someone talk like that? I just want to tell them to readjust their thinking and quit speaking things like that over themselves. You can be a healthy, vibrant, energetic ninety-five-year-old once you learn that you can have what you say. I remember when I turned forty-five (not that long ago, by the way), and people around me would joke about how I was getting old. I woke up on the morning of my birthday and the Lord said, "How old was your grandmother when she died?"

"In her late 90s," I said.

"You know," He said, "if you live even that long, you will still have your whole life to live over again."

And I thought, *Wow, that's true. I'm not even halfway there.* That was a great birthday present. I could have as much life remaining as the life I have already lived and without having to go through childhood, adolescence, and the whole maturing process again. I would begin with the level of experience I have now and live all that time over again, plus some. Why would I start to think I'm getting old? Why would I speak that about myself? If my words are life and death, then I certainly don't want to declare old age for myself before I'm even close to it. Stop yourself if you ever hear yourself saying things like this:

- "I am so tired all the time."
- "I must be getting old."
- "I'm so bored, I'm so lonely, I'm always so discouraged."
- "I'm hopeless with things like this. I never do well in situations like that."
- "Things never seem to work out for me."
- "I hate my job. My workplace is so oppressive."
- "I'm sick and tired of this."
- "This always happens to me."

When we understand the power of our words, then common phrases like this are no longer comfortable to say, as we recognize that we are inadvertently speaking negative things into being. The more you say, the more you are creating the conditions that make it true. That's not only how it works with your self-talk, but it applies to your words about others too. Those kinds of words add to the problem rather than being the solution.

Daryl Crawford-Marshall talks about us being called to be "prophetic solutionists." I love that. I think we should all be speaking as prophetic solutionists, declaring the answers rather than restating the problems. We'll talk in more detail later about why being problem focused is a very natural tendency for us, but not at all how God has designed us to work. The bottom line is that we are not helping anything when we simply reiterate the difficulties we are already experiencing. I'm not suggesting we lie about them; I am suggesting, however, that we speak of them only in solution-oriented terms. Start speaking life. Talk about how you are full of power by the Holy Spirit and how you are full of His strength, His joy, and His healing. Say what you already know to be true: that no weapon formed against you will prosper, that by Jesus' stripes you are healed, that life with Him is always increasing in abundance. Don't waste your words talking about what you feel to be the facts at the moment. Use them to declare what you know to be true for all of eternity and change your future with your words.

CHANGE THE WAY YOU THINK

Before we continue, let me be very clear about a couple of things. First, this is not a magic formula.

This is just not about being able to get what you want; it's about partnering with the Holy Spirit to bring about His purposes for your life and the world around you. That will certainly include seeing many of the desires of your heart fulfilled, so it is very satisfying and encouraging personally. But it is also bigger than your own goals. It is God's way of bringing His kingdom to earth through His people.

Second, don't make the mistake of just trying it for a few days and then deciding it doesn't work and giving up. Think of it more as sowing seeds. Some will sprout up pretty quickly. Others may go through long seasons before they bear fruit. I'm seeing some things today that I started declaring fifteen or twenty years ago. I'm also seeing the fruit of words I began declaring a few days ago. There is no formula to this; it's a divine process that works out in relationship with God. Don't lose heart.

Most importantly, though this is God's will for your life, be aware that it doesn't happen by accident. You won't stumble into it. You will have to discipline yourself to do it. It begins by retraining your thinking. Words flow from our thoughts, so the heart and mind are where this begins. Out of the abundance of the heart, the mouth speaks (Matthew 12:34). This is the start of your transition from the pattern of the world into renewing your mind with the truth. It will become more natural as you go on, but begin by being very intentional to speak life over your own life, your spouse, your children, your extended family members, your friends, co-workers, acquaintances, and every sphere of influence you have. Instead of talking about how difficult or dark or oppressing some obligation or relationship might be, talk about how you are the fragrance of Christ, and His Spirit goes with you into every corner of your world to bring light and life into it. Declare that the Lord is your strength, and with Him, there's nothing you can't do. Talk about how your home or your workplace is getting brighter and brighter, filled more and more with the glory of God. Jesus is in you, and wherever you go He is being released there through your words when you have conditioned yourself to speak life.

So ask yourself: what are you creating with your words? As I mentioned, I've been partnering with God to create with my tongue for most of the last two decades, and I am seeing things unfold now that I spoke years ago. It's really remarkable. We are called in the Holy Spirit to see and to say and then we will experience what we've seen and said. Throughout the rest of this book, we will look at plenty of Scriptural examples of how God tells those who are barren to sing with joy and those who are burdened to rejoice in their freedom. He wants us to go ahead and get happy about already having received the miracles and blessings we do not yet see with our natural eyes. Why? Because that makes us a lot like Him. We are made in the image of God, who calls things that are not as though they are, who named Abraham the father of many nations before he ever had a son. He has not changed. He invites us to enter into what He did in the pages of Scripture and what He is still doing in many lives now. He wants us to declare what He is saying, to create with our words and to speak life.

2

THE
CONVERSATION
IN HEAVEN

ALIGNING YOUR
WORDS WITH GOD'S

I got a new computer not long ago. I took it out
of the package, opened it up, and with the help of
my husband, went through the process of initiating
the setup and customizing it for my use. I knew how
to use it, at least the basics of creating documents,
using the Internet, getting connected on social
media, and all the other things we normally do with

our computers. But I also knew that this remarkable machine could perform a lot more functions than I knew how to use. It had all sorts of programs and capabilities waiting for me, lots of benefits that I could only learn over time, a world of potential for my fingertips to discover. So even though I could use it right away, I realized I needed to become much more acquainted with it to get the full benefit.

That's similar to how it is with the life God has given us too. We can experience it right away and walk in many of the blessings God has given us, but there is always more. We have been given everything pertaining to life and godliness (2 Peter 1:3), and we just need to unpack this life and figure out what we have. We have to learn what it means to live in Christ and to let Him live in us, so that we can walk out the truth that it is no longer we who live but Christ who lives in us. It takes practice to wake up every day and reckon ourselves dead to sin and alive to God in Christ, to look in the mirror of His face and of His Word and realize how that gaze transforms us. It's a supernatural life, and God is always calling us to step further into it. We can keep using the basics of this powerful life if we choose, or we can explore all the benefits that are promised to us. We have everything pertaining to life and godliness through the knowledge of Him. In other words, the more we become intimately acquainted with God in relationship, the more we manifest Jesus in our lives. God has given us full access to the kingdom and has a table spread before us in the presence of our enemies, but it is up to us to get up, see what is available, and eat it.

The power of our words is one of those capabilities waiting for us to unpack and learn to use. Our lives can be satisfied by the fruit of our mouths (Proverbs 18:20). We can have what we say. This principle is true whether we are intentional about it or not, but usually we get mixed fruit because both bad and good words come through our lips. If we learn to discipline our speech, however, we find a much more satisfying fruitfulness. We begin to see many of our desires being fulfilled simply because we have trained ourselves to talk about them in the right way.

SEEING DESIRES FULFILLED

God gives us the desires of our hearts. He makes that promise in several places in Scripture; one of the best known is Psalm 37:4, where He tells us that if we delight in Him, He gives us what we long for.

The problem for many of us is not knowing for sure whether our desires are good or not, whether they are from ourselves, from the devil, or from God. There's an easy way to relieve those worries, of course. If we go and have a talk with the Father about them, saturating ourselves in His presence, letting Him hug us and experience His love, He will bring our godly desires to the surface. We measure them in comparison to Scripture, and if they line up with His character and Word, we really have nothing to be concerned about. God gives us the desires of our heart. Christ in you is not dreaming of just surviving. He desires that you do the same works that He did and greater works. He wants to do exceedingly abundantly above all you can ask, hope, or imagine (Ephesians 3:20), and His invitation for you to partner with Him often comes in the form of a God-given desire.

I've seen far too many Christians question their God-given desires, as if a desire to see miracles and blessings is somehow selfish, proud, or wrongfully ambitious. If someone has a burning desire to see the paralyzed walk in the name of Jesus, there's really no need to agonize about whether it's the will of God. That's the sort of thing we see very clearly in His Word. Healing the sick certainly isn't something the devil would desire, and it doesn't seem very selfish. That's what Jesus did, and it fits the promises He gave to His followers, that they would do the works that He did and even greater works (John 14:12). These are the kinds of signs that follow those who believe. So, if you're dreaming about the lame walking, the blind seeing, the captives set free, the Word going forth in power, and more, you can know that's a God-given desire of your heart. You have full permission to speak it out, thank God for bringing it to pass (even in advance), and declare it done. Speak creatively. Whatever the Holy Spirit is revealing to your inspired imagination, He wants you to begin to speak it out.

I realize it is possible to have desires that don't align with God's Word so clearly, but He will always help you sort those questions out when you ask. Through knowing Him, His character, and His will in the Word of God, we train ourselves to discern good and evil. The Holy Spirit is your ever-present help in time of need and wants to help you be intimately acquainted with the Father and the Son. Even when you aren't sure about some of the things you are contemplating, you can be sure about the promises in the Word. I love praying the apostolic prayers from Scripture, especially those powerful prayers in

Ephesians 1 and 3 and Colossians 1, where Paul lays out in some detail the prayers he has for the people who read his letters. These are unquestionably God's will for each of us, our families, our friends, our co-workers, our neighbors, our fellow church members, our leaders, and everyone else we know. We have a remarkable opportunity not only to pray these things for others but also to go ahead and declare them as facts and thank God in advance for having done them. It's a powerful statement of faith to thank Him for things we don't yet see but have been promised through His Word. Speaking them forth makes that faith audible and tangible, and our words accomplish God's purposes. As you become intentional about your prayers and declarations, you begin to see a lot of your desires manifest in your actual experience.

The enemy would love you to believe that you have a bad heart and bad motives, but if you believe that you have died with Christ, then self is no longer relevant. When you have the mind of Christ, it is no longer you who lives, but Christ who lives in you; therefore, you can believe you have His motives. As a man thinks in his heart, so is he. If you believe yourself to have a sinful heart, you will be hampered by condemnation, but if you believe you are the righteousness of God in Christ, you will have faith to live righteously. If our hearts don't condemn us, we have confidence toward God and whatever we ask we receive (1 John 3:21–22). As we read His Word, we discover the truth about Him and the truth about us as new creations. As He is so are we in this world.

THE CONVERSATION IN HEAVEN

One of the reasons declarations are so powerful is that they create an alignment between our hearts and words and the conversation that is going on in heaven. Romans 8 tells us that the Holy Spirit is making intercession on our behalf (verses 26–27). He is praying for us and inspiring our prayers. A few verses later, we are told that Jesus is at the right hand of the Father making intercession for us (verse 34). So both the Spirit and the Son are in a conversation with the Father on our behalf, praying in perfect harmony with the Father's will.

Can you imagine what that conversation must be like? I'm sure they aren't pleading with the Father and trying to twist His arm. There is no distinction between the Father's will for us and the will of Jesus and the Holy Spirit. I can't imagine them saying, "Oh, Father, please help Katherine, just this once.

She really needs Your help this week. I know we've been asking a lot for her, but just this once, could You pleeease give her some extra wisdom this one time?" No, that's the kind of conversation that takes place between people who aren't in full agreement and need to be convinced. The intercession within the Trinity is much more certain, something much more like a declaration than a question. If they're praying in perfect harmony with the will of the Father, they are not begging or pleading with Him to do something He does not want to do. Jesus and the Holy Spirit are praying in accordance with the will of the Father, declaring what He already has in His heart. Perhaps the conversation goes something like this: "It's so wonderful, Father, that Katherine is part of our family. Help her to fully realize how loved and accepted she is today. It's so exciting that You have laid up good works in advance for this one to do this week. Help her wake up to the reality of what is available for her." Or something very much like that.

So our prayers are actually not a monologue. We enter into that conversation, as part of the family, aligning our words with the will of heaven as people who have been joined with Him. We have been born of the Holy Spirit by faith in Jesus and the will of the

Father. We are not outsiders. We don't have to pray like orphans, pleading for the Father to change His mind. He wants us to pray like He prays and then speak with His authority. He wants us to say, "Your will be done on earth as it is in heaven," fully aware of what His will is when we say it.

Think of all the ways that this truth applies to your prayers and conversations. If the Father, the Son, and the Holy Spirit are in perfect harmony in their conversations about you, the people you know, and the circumstances you face, they are declaring what has already been planned. They aren't pleading for breakthrough with your finances or your health. They are declaring what has already been provided before the foundation of the world for your provision and healing. Before you ever had a need, before you ever got sick, the Father had already gone before you to forgive your sins, heal your diseases, and restore your life. Jesus was already bruised, whipped, and pierced for your redemption and restoration. When we receive His salvation by faith, we have access to all these blessings. So the Son and the Holy Spirit are in heaven saying, "By the stripes of Jesus, this one is healed. Thank You, Father, that You already provided for their healing before the enemy ever came to afflict them. You already made a way. You always lead them in triumph. Help them to pick up the sword of the Spirit and fight with the words of life. Help them to tune in to the frequency of heaven and sing the truth on earth as it is in heaven." That means They are celebrating and declaring the will of the Father on your behalf.

What's left to do? Our words need to align with Theirs. That is the missing link. God's will is being done in heaven because They are declaring it, but a representative on earth needs to agree with Them for His will to be done here. Like tuning forks, God then wants us to begin resonating with the same conversational frequency of the Godhead so that we have perfect harmony on earth as it is in heaven. As His children, God wants us to talk like Him. Faith is the currency of God's kingdom, and words are actually a manifestation of faith. Our mouths speak what our hearts believe. When we understand that, we begin to speak differently. All of our speech becomes a matter of aligning ourselves with the perspective of the Father, the Son, and the Holy Spirit, of entering into Their conversation to declare things on earth that They want to do. God's kingdom advances on earth through the prayers, words, and faith of His people.

Our mouths speak what
our hearts believe.

Can you see why Scripture so often urges us to speak intentionally, to be careful about what we say, and to declare things for which we will actually enjoy the fruit? *"A word fitly spoken is like apples of gold in settings of silver" (Proverbs 25:11)*. A word can bring life or death. Some people forget the power they have and blurt out everything that pops into their head. If this applies to you, then this is a habit I would strongly counsel you to stop. A wise believer filters their thoughts and their words through the Word of God. They become vehicles for carrying out His will on earth.

What about when you don't know God's will? The Bible gives us a solution for that. There are many benefits that come with praying in tongues, but one of them is being able to voice God's will on earth even when we aren't sure what it is. Look at how The Passion Translation expresses Romans 8:26–27:

In a similar way, the Holy Spirit takes hold of us in our human frailty to empower us in our weakness. For example, at times we don't even know how to pray, or know the best things to ask for. But the Holy Spirit rises up within us to super-intercede on our behalf, pleading to God with emotional sighs too deep for words. God, the searcher of the heart, knows fully our longings, yet he also understands the desires of the Spirit, because the Holy Spirit passionately pleads before God for us, His holy ones, in perfect harmony with God's plan and our destiny.

The Holy Spirit fills our mouths with words and sounds that fit the conversation in heaven, and even when we don't understand what we are saying, we are declaring the Father's will on earth as it is in heaven.

Jude describes praying in the Holy Spirit as a means of building ourselves up in faith and keeping ourselves rooted in the Father's love (Jude 20–21). As we pray in tongues, the Holy Spirit increases our capacity to receive God's love and helps us supernaturally comprehend it. Even if we are operating under clouds of confusion or without awareness of what God is doing, He prays through us with power, bypassing any intruding thoughts of the enemy and any clutter in our own minds. He prays through us, about things that are not seen in the natural realm. He unfolds mysteries to us. He knows the conversation in heaven and will align our prayers with it. Revelation is downloaded into our hearts and faith is stirred up. From that place of being rooted in love and sensing revelation, we pray His will by His inspiration and miracles happen. This is really a powerful weapon, and I believe many Christians use it far too infrequently. We are invited to enter into the heavenly conversation, and this is one of the most effective ways to do it.

KNOW YOUR IDENTITY, USE YOUR GIFTS

I've been marinating in Romans 8 for a while because it is such a rich chapter. I would highly recommend you spend some time in it too. Read it in every translation you can get your hands on and really dig into it. Memorize it, enjoy it, and let the Spirit of God reveal His love for you through it. Being aware of our ability to participate in the conversation of heaven, understanding the will of God for our lives, unlocking the gifts we've been given, and experiencing the fullness of God's purposes for our lives has a major impact on our identities. Through the sacrifice of Jesus, God transfers His perfect righteousness to everyone who believes, which qualifies us to enter into this heavenly conversation and declare God's will on earth. *For it is with your heart that you believe and are justified, and it is with your mouth that you profess your faith and are saved (Romans 10:10, NIV).*

We must have confidence in our position in Christ, in order to participate in the heavenly conversation. The major themes of this chapter in Romans are about living in the power of the Holy Spirit and understanding the destiny God has given us. Toward the end of the chapter, Paul ties it together like this:

> *He knew all about us before we were born and He destined us from the beginning to share the likeness of His Son. This means the Son is the oldest among a vast family of brothers and sisters who will become just like Him. Having determined our destiny ahead of time, He called us to Himself and transferred His perfect righteousness to everyone He called. And those who possess His perfect righteousness He co-glorified with His Son! (Romans 8:29–30, TPT)*

I love that rendering. Jesus transferred His perfect righteousness to everyone He called. He essentially became sin so that we could become righteous (2 Corinthians 5:21). Isaiah 53:5 says, *"He was wounded for our transgressions, He was bruised for our iniquities."* Transgressions and iniquities are two different words in Hebrew; the first refers to our sins, the second our crookedness. In the atonement, Jesus didn't just deal with our sins; He dealt with our crookedness, which included all the crooked places within us. So when we come to Him and receive Him by faith, He gives us His righteousness in exchange for all our sins, guilt, shame, and sinful nature. We get a brand-new nature, and if we will live in it, all our crookedness is gone. We get brand-new hearts with new motives, the nature and attributes of Christ, at work within us. The more we understand that, the more we begin to grow in the knowledge of Him and the more we begin to access everything we've been given, which includes everything pertaining to life and godliness.

The passage goes on to explain our standing before God:

> *God has proved His love by giving us His greatest treasure, the gift of His Son. And since*

God freely offered Him up as the sacrifice for us all, He certainly won't withhold from us anything else He has to give. Who then would dare to accuse those whom God has chosen in love to be His? God Himself is the judge who has issued His final verdict over them "Not guilty!" (Romans 8:32–33, TPT)

He assures us that we've been made clean. We're holy. Even if our hearts condemn us, He is greater than our hearts (1 John 3:20). We are declared "not guilty." You may not feel like this is true, but the just live by faith, not by feelings. You can tell your feelings to get in line because the good news is that we are free from guilt and shame. You can preach to your soul, just like David did (Psalm 42:5, 11, 43:5). You can command your soul to bless the Lord and remember all His benefits (Psalm 103:1–5). You aren't crooked anymore, and you are not an outsider in God's throne room. You have been given holiness, righteousness, purity, and the joy of salvation. He has healed all your diseases. He is leading you in triumph. He is better than you think you deserve.

Scripture gives us a wonderful illustration of this in the book of Acts. Peter was on the roof having a rest, spending some time with God. He was probably making his requests known to God, as we are invited to do. He invites us to cast our cares on Him and thank Him for the answers, and He promises that His peace will guard our hearts and minds in Christ Jesus (Philippians 4:6–7). When we do that, we can just spend time with Him, gazing on His beauty and resting in His presence. Peter went to the rooftop to pray and was enjoying God's presence. In those precious moments of fellowship, we find that God often downloads His own desires. The things that are on His "prayer list" that He wants us to pray. I sometimes imagine what was happening that day with Peter. God said, "Peter, there are a few things on My mind. Let's get the Gentiles saved." And so God gave Peter a vision of unclean things and told him to eat. Peter, like all good Jews, had always avoided unclean foods. He protested. *"Not so, Lord! For I have never eaten anything common or unclean" (Acts 10:14).* God showed him the vision three times and convinced him that He was doing something new: *"What God has made clean you must not call unclean" (Acts 10:15).* Peter would need to put this into practice soon, as Gentiles were on their way to visit, and it would have been impossible to show hospitality without eating at the same table with them. God had a greater purpose than just the next interaction was going to have. When Peter met Cornelius, a Gentile centurion, he told him, "God has shown me that I should not call any man common or unclean." Peter was also speaking about us. We are not to call unclean whatever God has made clean.

But we do that all the time, don't we? God has declared us clean, and then we go about thinking of ourselves as unclean. He has made us saints, yet we so often continue to consider ourselves sinners. We know we've been forgiven, but then we've made mistakes since then. A voice tells us we need to feel guilty for a while and that we need to sit in the naughty corner or beat ourselves up a little bit more. It's as though, we think, the mercy of God only applies when we first get saved. We have been deceived into thinking we must work to receive forgiveness after we have been saved for a while. We have to remember: God suffered before we ever sinned. He knew everything you or I would do and still chose to pay the price ahead of time, so He could declare over us in heaven, "Not guilty!" So if the Father is declaring that you are not guilty, it really is not your place to say otherwise. You are holy, righteous, and clean. Yes, it is important that we acknowledge and repent of our sins, but He is faithful and just to forgive you of your sin when you confess it. He throws it into the sea of His forgetfulness and declares us to be cleansed of all unrighteousness (1 John 1:9). So when you think you should pay for your sin for a while or feel the emotional weight of it just a bit longer, you need to realize that won't work. You can't pay for your sin. Jesus was punished for your sin so you would not have to be punished for it. It isn't your sacrifice that pleases God; it's your faith in His sacrifice. Anything else is pride.

That's wonderful news! The "not guilty" definition is permanent. Romans 8 continues with the implications for us:

> *Who then is left to condemn us? Certainly not Jesus, the Anointed One! For He gave His life for us, and even more than that, He has conquered death and is now risen, exalted and enthroned by God at His right hand. So how could He possibly condemn us since He is continually praying for our triumph? (Romans 8:34, TPT)*

Jesus does not want us to live a life of condemnation, fear, and shame. He doesn't want us talking about ourselves negatively, which is something we will discuss, in more detail, in the next chapter. He doesn't want us defining ourselves by our performance. For a born-again believer, that is unbelief. If you have believed in Jesus, recognized that you need the mercy of God, and received His grace, you are covered with His grace. There is no condemnation for those who are in Christ; that's how this great chapter in Romans began. He has made you righteous.

When we have received that gift, we need to walk in the revelation of this truth daily so we can experience the joy and freedom that comes from salvation. We have the blessings of salvation even when we aren't aware of them, but we cannot actually experience them unless we are consciously living by faith in them. We have to apply what we know because God wants us to live in supernatural joy and continual peace. When you feel like a hypocrite . . . when you don't feel qualified to walk in supernatural power . . . when your guilt or shame is keeping you from even going to church . . . God is waiting for you to come into agreement with heaven. He has given you the keys of His kingdom, and He is inviting you into the conversation between the Father, the Son, and the Holy Spirit. He wants you to hear what They are praying so you can agree with it, declare it by faith, and see it come to pass on earth.

That is a powerful gift, and far too many Christians are letting it go to waste. God is calling us to enter into His gates, hear the divine conversation, and say, "Your will be done for my life, for my family, for my church, my workplace, my community, on earth as it is in heaven." Then you can go forth in supernatural power carrying the aroma of Christ into your world, manifesting the glory of God, and declaring life, godliness, health, wisdom, prosperity, blessing, and fruitfulness.

If you're self-conscious about God giving you so much attention and lavishing you with so many gifts and promises, it's time to get over it! You are the apple of His eye. You are intensely loved beyond your ability to understand it. One of Paul's apostolic prayers says this love is so beyond our comprehension that we have to be given supernatural power to be able to know it (Ephesians 3:16–19). Yet God is delighted to open our eyes and our hearts to it. He wants us to be overwhelmed with it. He is so loving and kind.

That is the message of Romans 8. We are lovers of God who have been called to fulfill His purpose. He knew us, called us, and destined us before we were born to share the likeness of Jesus. He is leading us in victory and into places of glory. Also, He has called us to open our mouths to know the truths of His kingdom, declare His purposes for the world around us, and speak life over ourselves and everyone we know.

.

3

SPEAK LIFE OVER YOURSELF

STEPPING INTO YOUR TRUE IDENTITY

I started a new teaching position at a Christian school years ago, and during teacher orientation, we were sent away for fifteen minutes to ask the Lord what He was saying about us and to listen for an answer. Once I got alone with Him, I asked Him directly. "Lord, talk to me. I know I have things that need to change. What do You want to tell me? What do You want to fix?" My paper and pencil were ready.

"I love you," He said.

That didn't excite me very much. "I know, Lord. That's basic. Really, what do You want to say? My heart is wide open. I can take it."

Again, I heard the same thing. "I love you."

I sighed. What was I going to tell all the others when we got back together to share what we heard? "Lord, everybody already knows You love everybody. We get that. I want to go deeper with You. I'm giving You access to my heart. What do You want to change in me?"

"I love you."

I was so frustrated. I was going to have to report to the other teachers that all I could hear in fifteen minutes of listening was a basic Christian truth.

What I didn't realize in the moment was that these were the words I needed to hear more than anything else. God wanted me to know that He wasn't waiting to correct me. His priority for me was not to let me know all the things He didn't like about me and wanted to change. People may have agendas like that, but God doesn't. In fact, Jesus said He did not come into the world to condemn it but to save it

(John 3:17). He actually believes His own promises for us, such as it's no longer we who live but Christ who lives in us (Galatians 2:20), that He has taken our crookedness and made it straight (remember that's what "iniquities" refers to in Isaiah 53:5 and Psalm 103:3). As I said earlier, our transgressions are our sins, but our iniquities are our crookedness. Jesus was wounded for our transgressions and bruised for our iniquities; the chastisement for our peace was on Him, and by His stripes we are healed (Isaiah 53:5). When Jesus was crucified on our behalf, He said, *"It is finished" (John 19:30).* This is not something that happens over time. We already have access to every blessing He has promised us. We are new creations. So the Father's heart toward us is not focused on everything that has gone wrong that needs to be fixed. It's on what He has done in us. He is waiting for us to come into agreement with what He believes about us. He is waiting for us to receive His "I love you." Only then will we be empowered to live out His righteousness. Only then can we walk and speak in His power.

Proverbs 23:7 tells us that what goes on in our hearts will shape us. *"As a man thinks within himself, so is he."* This verse is quoted often, but I'm not sure we take it as seriously as we need to. At the very least, it tells us we need to be vigilant about the things we allow into our heads. Our self-talk and our vision matter because our thoughts inevitably become the basis of our words.

Do you have a vision for yourself? By that, I mean more than whatever you are planning to do or what your dreams are for your life. More specifically, do you have a vision of what you are really like? Does that vision line up with what God says about you?

Most of us think we know what we are really like, and it often isn't a very flattering picture. It's also usually wrong. Scripture tells us what our true nature is in Christ. When we recognize our need for God's forgiveness, believe that Jesus is our Savior, and surrender our lives to Him, we become new creations. We accept the fact that Jesus became sin on our behalf so we could become His righteousness. He became what we were so we could become what He is. Now we have not only mercy and forgiveness but also eternal life. We actually become the righteousness of God in Christ (2 Corinthians 5:21). Everything we love about God now becomes true of us. He is love? So are we. Is love patient and kind? Then so are we. *"As He is, so are we in this world" (1 John 4:17).* Therefore, we are patient and kind. We are a manifestation of God's love in this world. That's our new definition.

If that doesn't fit your experience, it's not because it isn't true. It's because you don't yet think this way in your heart. You haven't yet believed the amazing truths God says about you. Before we rush into the day's events, we need to get a vision of what we are becoming and what our behavior should look like that day. It's stewardship of the divine nature within us. Many people get up in the morning with a negative self-definition already in their hearts: they are tired and cranky, in a bad mood, stressed about the day, dreading the circumstances coming their way. Thoughts like that will rush into your mind if you let them. If you don't take control of them right away, they will set up camp and keep running through your mind. Instead, you have to take them captive, cast them down, and replace them with truth. You separate what you feel from what you know to be true according to God's Word. You don't walk by feelings; you walk by faith. You speak life over yourself.

For me, that looks something like this: "I am the righteousness of God by faith. I am strong and healthy. I am patient and kind. I am loved and I am loving. When I talk to people, I am secure and confident in Christ. I am rooted and grounded in the love of God, and I spread the aroma of His love to everyone I meet. I drink continuously from the river of His pleasure for me. I know He loves me and shows me His favor. I know His plan is to prosper me, to give me hope and a future. I am blessed, favored, and adored by My Father. I never have to compare myself to anyone else or feel jealous or competitive because my Father has a beautiful life designed just for me. I have my Father's Word, His promises, and His assurance. He will never let me down, no matter what my circumstances look like. Because Christ now lives in me, I am a blessing everywhere I go and a gift to everyone I meet." All of those statements come from biblical truths that tell us who we are and how we relate to our Father.

If you say something like that over yourself every day, you will see some amazing changes. Conversely, if you don't have a positive vision for yourself, this principle from Proverbs about the way we think in our hearts becomes nothing more than an empty concept. You don't get to receive the benefits of it if you let negative thoughts run randomly through your head. To experience the power of this principle, you have to apply the wisdom you have and discipline yourself to think the thoughts God has for you.

Discipline is not a bad word. It's actually the fruit of the Spirit called self-control. God has empowered us to choose not to be moved by every feeling and thought. We can choose instead to fill our hearts and minds with the right things and lay hold of all that God has for us. Every day we have a choice whether to apply truth to our lives or not. We can tell our souls what to think and feel. We can choose to bless God and to speak life over ourselves. Once we have learned to speak life over ourselves, we are in a position to speak life into others. But it all begins with how we see ourselves.

Scripture tells us this again and again. We are only able to love because God first loved us (1 John 4:19).

Jesus commands us to love one another as we love ourselves (Mark 12:31), which is a real problem if we don't love ourselves very much. If you don't see yourself as righteous, holy, and pure (as defined by God), you will not walk in these truths, and you will probably judge yourself very harshly. And if you judge yourself harshly, you will likely turn that condemnation outward and judge everyone else harshly too. That's why it's so important to take captive those thoughts that are trying to rob you of the peace and joy of your salvation and fill your mind instead with the thoughts of God, as He has revealed them. Thank Him for who He says you already are. Meditate on your new identity. Begin to speak it out. It won't make you arrogant; it will actually bring you to a place of such gratitude that you'll hardly have enough time to express it. You will begin to realize how good and kind He has been toward you and how delighted He is in His love for you. Your heart will open up to recognize even more of His goodness and receive even more of His love and it will lead to an absolute transformation in the heart. You won't want to sin anymore because it will be so intrusive and disruptive in your relationship with Him. You will become in experience what God has been saying about you all the time.

When you think bad things about yourself and believe lies that contradict what God has done in you, coming to God in gratitude and worship will seem more like an obligation or a religious duty. But joy will come through meditating on the truth of God's Word, and He wants you to overflow with that joy. This is what happens when we cultivate a lifestyle of agreeing with the Word of God. When you can truly worship Him for the new identity He has given you, through His love and mercy, you will start to get really happy about things. As you believe in your heart, so you will become.

THE LIES YOU HEAR

If we don't know who we are and aren't declaring what God is saying about us, we will be vulnerable to whatever other people are saying about us. Human nature looks to someone outside of ourselves to define us (if not God, then other people), so we easily let other voices become our reality. We can only walk in truth when we know what God says about us and line our words up with His. He wants you to know that when you have surrendered your life to Christ, you are cleansed of all unrighteousness and have become the righteousness of God in Christ. You received a new heart and a new nature the moment you put your faith in Jesus as the Redeemer. Start declaring, you can do all things through Him who strengthens you (Philippians 4:13). Statements like, "I can't do this; I'm sick and tired of this; I can't go on like this," are all contradictions to what His Word says about you. Why would you want to say such things? What good can come of stating what may appear to be true but is not the true reality of our new lives? God asks us to call those things that are not, as though they are. Faith is the assurance of things hoped for, the evidence of things not seen. Declare the unseen in faith if you want to begin walking in it.

The problem for most of us, at some point in our lives, is a running commentary going on in our heads that dwells on lies instead of truth. A lot of people have some pretty awful self-talk: "You idiot, what did you do that for? You're so lazy. You never get it right. You'll always be like this. Everything is going wrong. Things never work out for me." Your internal conversation with yourself is an indication of how well you are trusting God and loving yourself. When your thoughts have this flavor to them, you will be limited in the power you walk in and the love you are able to give others. Jesus tells us to love others as we love ourselves. Loving yourself is not being arrogant. If we dislike or even hate ourselves, this is a lie of the devil who's trying to destroy us. It is hurtful to God who created you and damaging to yourself. Having any destructive feelings about ourselves makes it difficult to love others fully. Hating yourself is not going to be helpful to anyone. Your decision to agree with how God feels about you and to receive His love is the level at which you will be able to love others. If you are continually self-deprecating, critical, and harsh on yourself, then this is the way you will inevitably behave toward others. In other words, your negative self-talk not only hurts you but negates your capacity to love others. When you speak kindly to yourself and encourage yourself with positive inner talk, you will naturally start to speak to others and encourage them in the same way. Your ability to love and your ability to walk in the power of God starts here. You need to start agreeing with God's love, hopes, and plans for you and start prophesying to yourself. God (who is the King and our Papa) wants you to live like the royal son or daughter you now are, a prince or princess of His kingdom. When someone adopts a child here on earth, that child becomes their completely legal son or daughter and their heir. The same has happened to us in God's family. This not only brings you in line with the truth about yourself as God defines you but equips you to prophesy His love and truth to others.

> *Nothing is more appealing than speaking beautiful life-giving words. For they release sweetness to our souls and inner healing to our spirits. (Proverbs 16, TPT)*

Declare the unseen in faith if you want to begin walking in it.

It isn't easy to retrain your mind in the right thought patterns, especially if this kind of negative self-talk has been going on for years. The pathways in your brain may have grown deep ruts in some negative directions. The enemy is a chatterbox, and he always has something deceptive or destructive to say. The good news is that it is always possible to take your thoughts captive. If your thoughts, about yourself or your situation, are exalting themselves against the knowledge of God, it is time to cast them down! In other words, any thought you have about yourself (that isn't true about God) is a lie, and it's trying to deceive you about your identity because you are now "as Christ is in this world" (1 John 4:17, paraphrased). You cannot afford to walk around with negative, unforgiving, destructive, nasty thoughts in your head. If you don't get rid of them, they will grow roots of bitterness, resentment, and unforgiveness. Don't just prune them; rip them out by the roots! If you encountered an intruder in your house, you would have something to say about it. It would be a pretty strong reaction. So, when you find a thief in your soul, you can't just let it camp there. Don't tolerate the liar that is sitting on your shoulder and whispering deceptive and destructive thoughts in your ear!

You have to do two things to get rid of them: take them captive and replace them with truth. We are told that *"the weapons of our warfare are not carnal but mighty in God for pulling down strongholds, casting down arguments and every high thing that exalts itself against the knowledge of God, bringing every thought into captivity to the obedience of Christ" (2 Corinthians 10:4–5).* Once you've recognized the real source of destructive thoughts, tell them to stop! Just as Jesus calmed a storm by commanding it to cease, you can speak to the thoughts in your mind and tell them they have to go. Cast them down, take them captive, and refuse to let them continue! That isn't the end of the process; if you don't replace them with something better, the lying thoughts will come back again. So fill the places those lying thoughts occupied with some new and true ones: "Jesus is in me and I am in Him. I have the mind and the motives of Christ. I love like He loves. I'm as pure as God is pure. I am free from sin, clean, and whole. There is no stain in me. He has separated my sin from me as far as the east is from the west. He keeps no record or remembrance of it. In fact, it's no longer I who live, but Christ who lives in me. My conscience, my mind, my heart, and my body are clean. No matter how bad my sins were, I am a new person from the inside out because Jesus has made me new. I forgive myself, just as He has forgiven me. Now, because God is love, I can declare that I too am love personified, patience in the flesh, the embodiment of kindness. Where I was once unholy and unable to fellowship with God, I am now completely holy through faith in His grace and am fully in fellowship with Him." That's the only way to deal with the lies you hear. Not only do they need to go but truth needs to come. The atmosphere starts to shift because you are actually doing spiritual warfare when you make declarations.

I was on a flight returning from Israel to Zurich, and I was going through a really difficult season. I had just been through a big scare with my health, and for some reason, I was overcome with fear on the plane that night. This was out of character for me; I'm not normally filled with negative thoughts so suddenly. I became so afraid of the negative scenarios beginning to play out in my head that I began to cry quietly in my seat. I prayed, "God help me, talk to me, please help me." This went on for a while and then the plane landed.

I got off the plane, walked up the gangplank, and the first sign I saw in the airport was a big advertisement for an investment bank. The only words on it, in big bold print, were: "Am I a good father?" It was a picture of a man with his head in his hands, thinking about whether he was making the right decisions for his family. The context of the message wasn't what mattered to me because there was an unmistakable different message in it for me. I felt the Father put His arm around me and say, "Katherine, am I a good Father? You know I am. I'll take care of you. You have nothing to worry about. I love you and I am with you always."

This is the sort of relationship God has with us. We don't have to pretend we have it all together. In our weakness, He loves to be strong. In our fear, He delights in manifesting His goodness and casting all our fear out with His love. He wants to speak hope-filled words to us. He wants to be closer to you than any other person is, even your spouse and closest family members. No human being can give you what He wants to give you. You can live in complete confidence that you are utterly loved, perfectly safe in His arms, and never needing to walk alone.

That is the blessing of righteousness, complete peace and joy in the Holy Spirit, who is continually urging us to come into agreement with what heaven is saying about us. So, if that is His heart toward us, why would we repeat lies to ourselves? Why would we live in a negative mental environment that tears us down? We have to get out from under those deceptions and agree with what Scripture says, no matter what we think we see in our past or our present circumstances. We have to let God define truth for us and then align our words with what He says.

So what does God think about us? Scripture overflows with wonderfully encouraging statements about those who believe in Jesus, who have been forgiven and redeemed from their sins, and who are now new creations in Christ. Here is a very small sampling out of many, many verses I have found. I encourage you to say them out loud to yourself:

- I am a child of God (1 John 1:12).

- I am a friend of God (John 15:15).

- I'm not condemned by God (Romans 8:1).

- I am an heir with Jesus of all God's promises (Romans 8:17).

- I have wisdom, righteousness, and redemption in Christ (1 Corinthians 1:30).

- I am a new creation (2 Corinthians 5:17).

- I am the righteousness of God (2 Corinthians 5:21).

- I have been set free (John 8:36; Galatians 5:1).

- I have been blessed with every spiritual blessing (Ephesians 1:3).

- I am holy and blameless in God's sight (Ephesians 1:4).

- I am a citizen of heaven (Philippians 3:20).

- I am seated with Christ in heavenly places (Ephesians 2:6).

- I have everything pertaining to life and godliness and can receive God's promises and participate in His divine nature (2 Peter 1:2–3).

- As Jesus is, so am I in this world (1 John 4:17).

This list could go on and on. Because it's so important to speak truth to ourselves often, I've included these and many others at the end of this chapter. This is spiritual self-talk, and the more you say these things, the more you declare truth, the more your mind begins to embrace it and transform your words into genuine, powerful faith. I challenge you to search the Scriptures because there are so many more promises hidden for you to find.

Some Christians are so accustomed to the lies that it is difficult to believe the extravagant truths God tells us. We are chosen? Holy and beloved? The righteousness of God in Christ? "Wait a minute," our hearts want to tell us. "No one is holy but God." In the natural, that's true, but Jesus came and was crucified so our old lives could die, be buried with Him, and resurrected with Him into a new reality. He loved us so much that He exchanged His life for ours, becoming what we are, dying the death we deserved because of our sins, so we could receive everything He is and live in His eternal life.

So if we've received His life within us, we cannot be anything but holy and good. We may not act holy and good all the time, but those actions are not defining our new reality. God is the one who defines us, and He chooses to define us by Jesus when we believe in and accept Him. So that when God looks at you, He doesn't see someone who is separated from Him, but one who has been joined to Him. You are His very own child now. You have been washed in the blood of Jesus; you now have the Spirit of Jesus, the resurrected life of Jesus, the name of Jesus, the authority of Jesus, the mind of Jesus, the heart and motives of Jesus, and the identity of Jesus. You have been joined to Him as one, like a husband to his beloved bride. Therefore, you are holy and blameless in Him. The righteous live by faith, so you have to believe this, then you'll enjoy the blessing and fruit of it. It's true whether you are fully experiencing it right now or not. You are a member of His body and a partaker in His promises. You can have boldness and confident access to God through faith in Christ. You have been made complete, and you are more dearly loved than you can imagine.

So when I went to the Lord at that teacher orientation and asked Him to speak to me, I really didn't need to expect a commandment, a rebuke, or an overhaul, did I? I needed this word about the completeness and comprehensiveness of His love. We don't have to be afraid that God is going to growl at us and remind us of all our sins. He has thrown all our sins into a sea of forgetfulness, and I like to think the biggest ones sink the fastest! He remembers our sin no more (Hebrews 8:12)! God is kinder than we feel like we deserve. He now invites us to agree with Him in faith minute by minute, day after day, year after year, forever.

Do you realize what this means? If He is love personified and you are in Him and He in you, then you can be love personified. You *are* love. This is not a theory; it's an invitation. You are the patience of God, the kindness of God, the joy and delight of God. You don't have to try to be these things; you just are. Once you're saved, His words about you are actually your new definition. You don't strive for them; you receive them by faith, and then you grow into the experience of them as you believe. Whatever He is saying about us is what we need to be saying about ourselves, all the time.

Don't be surprised by the lies that come. The war is real. Those old thoughts will resurface from time to time: "You are sinful, you are lazy, you are not measuring up, you don't have a new heart after all, do you?" In 2 Corinthians 10:4 (which we looked at a few paragraphs ago), the Scripture reminds us that any thought we have about ourselves that tries to gain more attention than what God tells us, we have the choice to rebuke it. God gave us all a free will. Therefore, we can choose to take captive, cast down, and decisively replace these old, lying thoughts with God's truth. Do not compromise or negotiate with these lies! Just reject them completely, thoroughly, finally. They will sap you of your strength, your joy, and your holy confidence. God's truth about you will fill you with life. When you speak the Word of God, you are actually speaking life into yourself.

We are told that if our hearts do not condemn us, we have confidence before God, that whatever we ask, we receive (1 John 3:21–22). Because that is such a threatening truth to the enemy, he continually tries to get you to believe something else. He wants you to live in condemnation, in guilt, in the doubts that come from assuming you don't qualify for God's blessings and promises. Even when you get used to speaking truth to yourself, you have to continue the good fight because a battle rages over you every day. The enemy gets really nervous about the prospect of people who realize who they are in Christ and who walk in victory, truth, and power. He will surround you with lies about your identity, your circumstances, your future, and anything else that will distract you from the life God has designed for you to live. He will try to convince you that you are not qualified to walk in power; that no one today can lay hands on the sick in Jesus' name and watch them recover; that your words are only words and there is no real power in your tongue; that the authority Jesus gave you to trample on snakes and scorpions and over all the power of the enemy is just symbolic or abstract; that you are only seated with Christ in heavenly places theoretically perhaps, but not in any way that has practical value. Recognize that those thoughts are not coming from God! Whatever condemnation is included in the negative thoughts is not the conviction of the Holy Spirit because He will always bring you into God's promises through repentance and faith, rather than telling you that they are out of reach because of your unworthiness. Jesus has made you worthy. Period. The great cloud of witnesses is cheering you on to a life of impact that will last for generations. Our eternal life with Christ begins the moment we make that decision to invite Him into our lives forever. God wants you to live in perfect peace and abundant joy in every situation, regardless of what is going on around you. Any thought that leads you away from the righteousness, peace, and joy of the kingdom of God is not from the Holy Spirit. It is from the thief and needs to be dealt with emphatically.

If you do not deal with these lies decisively (if you tolerate them at all), they tend to multiply. They take root and, like a magnet, collect other thoughts that are attracted to that deceptive and condemning environment. They will sap you of energy, steal your joy, and drain the life out of you. You need to get rid of them quickly.

When I first got my smart phone, I didn't realize I was supposed to close all the applications I had opened. I would just click off one and open up another. Then I noticed that my battery power would go down more quickly than I thought it should. Tom looked at my phone and saw the reason. "You have a hundred applications open! If you don't close them, they will tick away in the background and drain your power and slow everything down." So he showed me how to swipe them up and off the screen. That's what happens with our negative thoughts when we let them keep running in the background. If we don't take them captive and swipe them off the screen of our minds, they will keep sapping our strength and stealing our joy. The way you swipe them away is to speak firmly to them: "No, that isn't true. I'm not tolerating that thought anymore. What God says about me is true, so that's what I'm going to think and speak." Don't even repeat what the enemy is saying. Just replace it with the truth of God's Word. It really is that simple.

Remember that as a man thinks in his heart, so is he. That makes this battle extremely important. Your sense of identity (not your true identity in Christ, but your life experience) is at stake. If you think you're useless, weak, foolish, sinful, ugly, or whatever else you might be believing, that's what will begin to manifest in your life. You will take on that persona and live it out in your relationships. For example, if you have an addiction and identify yourself with it, that addiction will stick with you. If you embrace a character flaw as part of your nature, it will bog you down and be very difficult to overcome. On the other hand, if you start to embrace what God says about you and begin saying those things yourself, you rewire your spirit (and even your brain) and begin to step into the reality in which God wants you to live. You don't dwell on who you were; you grow into who you are becoming. You live above the visible, not beneath it.

Some people, either with the look on their faces or their negative words, want to make sure everyone else knows how badly things are going for them. Sometimes they're just desperate for someone to tell them the opposite. They are often just trying to provoke an encouraging response. As uplifting as the words of other people can be, there's a better way to find encouragement than looking for it from others. Instead, shift your thinking. Decide that you are not going to be defined by how you feel or by your circumstance. Declare that you are going to be defined by the Word of God alone. Pick up the sword of the Spirit and use it. Don't prompt people to throw you a crumb occasionally when you tell them how terribly you're doing, hoping for them to contradict you. Choose not to stay down on the floor. Get up and speak life. When you start to move in the right direction, the Holy Spirit will move with you. He will help you fill your mouth with His words and prayers.

Remember that the weapons of your warfare are mighty for the pulling down of strongholds. As you speak words of truth, they are mighty in pulling down those harassing thoughts that weigh you down. When some intimidating thought about your future comes to mind, declare what God says about it: *"I know the thoughts that I think toward you, says the Lord, thoughts of peace and not of evil, to give you a future and a hope" (Jeremiah 29:11).* That is God's plan for you, His revealed will. If your mind is convinced of the enemy's plans for you, then you're going to have a miserable life and end up lonely. Reject any other contradictions to God's will by simply putting your hand up like a policeman would and say, "Stop it! In Jesus' name, get out!" Then declare the truth. According to God's revealed will for your life, you can call those things that be not as though they are and declare the truth. You are healthy. You are prosperous. You have abundant life. God's plans are to give you hope and a wonderful future. He is calling you into the works that Jesus did, and even greater works than those (John 14:12). You are called and anointed to manifest Jesus wherever you go. You are filled with faith, hope, love, and everything else God has put into your new spiritual DNA, in Christ. The truth is good and it always overcomes.

Declare it now:

- I am prosperous.

- I am healthy.

- I have hope and a great future ahead of me.

- God has great plans for me.

- I am qualified to do everything God has planned for me to do.

- I do the works of Jesus and greater works.

- I manifest Jesus everywhere I go.

- I am deeply loved.

SPEAK THE LANGUAGE OF POWER

Begin to speak the truths of the kingdom, starting with those concerning yourself. Your sin, your crookedness, your infirmities, your weaknesses, and your impurities are all gone. They have all been covered, removed, and replaced with the power of Jesus. Don't settle for anything less than what God has promised. Speak His promises often and with confidence. Declare your own righteousness, not according to what you've done but according to what

Jesus has done and what God has said. Apply the wisdom you have to edify yourself, building yourself up in the truths of God's Word. Let life flow out of your mouth in every situation you face.

When coaches tell their players to imagine scoring a goal, to envision making the right moves, to see themselves executing all their plays perfectly, they are not just employing psychological strategies. They are harnessing a biblical truth. This truth works in any situation, but it is so much more powerful when we align ourselves with eternal truth. Use the Word of God as a weapon and speak it in confidence and faith. In the next two chapters, we will discuss using it to bless others and to influence circumstances, but the first place to look is in the mirror at yourself. You need to experience the fullness of God in your own life before you can effectively bless others with His power and presence. Learn to speak words of life from the moment you get up in the morning. If you wake up feeling sick or tired, you will gain absolutely no benefit by saying what you are feeling. In fact, you will continue to have what you say. You will benefit greatly by intentionally changing the climate around you with your words: "This is the day that the Lord has made, I will rejoice and be glad in it. Jesus says in the Bible, 'I am the Lord who heals you.' I am full of joy in the Holy Spirit. The joy of the Lord is my strength. Jesus is living inside of me. I am happy, holy, and loved. I am full of the presence and power of God. I fully anticipate that the God, who is able to do exceedingly abundantly beyond all I can ask or think, will demonstrate His goodness to me again and again today. Thank You, Lord, for laying up good works in advance for me to do. Thank You for allowing me to carry the aroma of Christ wherever I go. Thank You that I am a child of the Most High. Thank You that I will be an awesome husband/wife/father/mother/brother/sister/co-worker/friend today. Even in my worst moments, You are forgiving, redeeming, restoring, and blessing me as well as the world around me, through the power that is at work in me." With words like these, you set the tone of your self-talk for the day and align your words with the truths of the kingdom.

Refuse to dwell on your sins. Repent and get on with your life. God has forgotten them and so must you. See yourself being the presence of Christ to those around you each day. Expect the blessing of the Lord to affect everyone you meet. There is nothing arrogant in these expectations. You don't have these promises because you deserve the power of God in your life; you have them because He lovingly gives it to you by His grace. It is His love gift to you.

When you are able to receive God's love and to love yourself this way, you become a vessel of His love and power for those around you. You cannot give out what you have not experienced yourself. We love because He first loved us (1 John 4:19). We are to love others as we love ourselves (Mark 12:31). People who have not been bathed in the love of God are often hard on themselves, and then try to cut others down in order to feel better. If you have been declaring truth over yourself, you will feel no need to do this. If you genuinely know you are a new creation, dead to sin and alive to God in Christ, defined by your identity in Jesus with the Spirit of God living and working within you, you will walk in ever-increasing power daily. It all begins by constantly telling yourself the truth. You will know the truth and the truth will set you free from the lies of the enemy.

DECLARATIONS
FOR YOUR LIFE

There is virtually no limit to the promises and blessings you can declare for yourself and others. You have what you say. Here are a few to get started:

- I am crucified with Christ; it is no longer I who live but Christ who lives in me (Galatians 2:20).

- I am in Jesus; He is in me; we are one (Colossians 1:17; Romans 8:1; John 17:20–23).

- I have the mind of Christ (1 Corinthians 2:16).

- I am the righteousness of God in Christ (2 Corinthians 5:21).

- I have been cleansed, forgiven, made new (Psalm 103:12; Titus 3:5).

- In Jesus, I am thoroughly loved, adored, treasured, and worthy to receive all of His blessings (1 John 3:1).

- With Jesus, I am an heir of all things. What belongs to Him now also belongs to me (Romans 8:17).

- I am a new creation. Old things have passed away; all things have become new (2 Corinthians 5:17).

- God is making all things new (Revelation 21:5).

- I am a child of the royal family, an heir of the royal estate (1 Peter 1:4).

- All of God's promises are yes and amen in Christ; I am in Christ; therefore, all of God's promises apply to me (2 Corinthians 1:20).

- Like Jesus, I walk in ever-increasing favor (Luke 2:52).

- I walk in divine health (Psalm 103:1-3; Isaiah 53:5).

- I live under supernatural protection (Psalm 91).

- I have authority to trample over all the power of the enemy (Luke 10:19).

- I have the keys of the kingdom (Matthew 16:19).

- I have everything pertaining to life and godliness and can receive God's promises and participate in His divine nature (2 Peter 1:2–3).

- It is God who is at work in me to will and to work for His good pleasure; therefore, the motives, purposes, and promises of God are growing in me (Philippians 2:13).

- Goodness and mercy follow me everywhere (Psalm 23:6).

- I am a child of God (1 John 1:12).

- I am a friend of God (John 15:15).

- I'm not condemned by God. He has made me righteous (Romans 8:1).

- I am free (John 8:36; Galatians 5:1).

- I have been blessed with every spiritual blessing (Ephesians 1:3).

- I am holy and blameless in God's sight (Ephesians 1:4).

- I am a citizen of heaven (Philippians 3:20).

- I am seated with Christ in heavenly places (Ephesians 2:6).

- As Jesus is, so am I in this world (1 John 4:17).

4

SPEAK LIFE OVER OTHERS

SEEING AND PROPHESYING DESTINIES

When one of my daughters was younger, she went through a time of wandering from the Lord, as many young people do when they are sorting out what they believe. I didn't always have a great attitude toward her during that time. I would struggle with judgmental thoughts about some of the choices she was making, all the things that didn't fit my vision for her life. I would smile at her on the outside, but on the inside, it was a different story. We would butt heads often, and I didn't feel we were very connected at a heart level. I thought I was doing all the right things, so I was surprised when I was talking with God and He told me my thoughts were defining her. I realized how I might be distorting her perception of Him. To whatever degree I was representing God to her, my judgment was causing her to put up a wall of defense not only to me but also to Him.

God challenged me to ask Him to show me the true picture of her, the person who she really was in the Spirit and how He saw her. As a new vision of her came to mind, I began to thank Him for her true identity. I began to think differently about her and see her from His perspective, as my sister in Christ who was worthy of respect, as someone walking in the fullness of her destiny. As I envisioned her in this new light, I began to treat her with the same respect I would give to someone who had been walking in spiritual maturity and serving God sacrificially for years. I spoke words of affirmation and honor to her. When I was alone with God, I would continue to declare the destiny He had planned for her and thank Him for fulfilling it. The walls began to come down.

She began to change. Over time, she turned back to the Lord, no longer feeling judged but knowing how much she was loved. It was a beautiful thing that only God could have done, but He did it by changing the way I saw and spoke.

SEEING TRUE IDENTITIES

When you realize who you are, you find it much easier to see who other people are and begin prophesying their identities and destinies over them. If your spouse or children or others in your life are not walking the way you want them to walk, instead of prophesying what you don't like (their "terrible attitude" or bad habits) start prophesying those things that are part of their God-given destiny. Declare things that are not, as though they already are. It will help to ask God for His vision of who they are becoming so you don't end up just prophesying your will for their lives. When God reveals something to you, go ahead and thank Him for it and declare it. Remember, your words are always prophesying, whether for good or for bad. Empower those around you to step into the destiny God wants and has for them by declaring it, on their behalf.

In order to do that, we will need to overcome a lot of our natural judgments. I believe God wants us to treat everyone with the love He has for them. Jesus was known as a friend of sinners. He did not get that reputation by walking around criticizing people. He looked past their current flaws to see their destinies and the Father's purposes for them. God wants us to love others like that. After all, that's how He loves us.

The more you experience that love, the more you are able to extend it to others. When we do the wrong thing, God doesn't tell us how upset He is and how He will just need some time to get over it. He comes running in, telling us how holy and blameless we are, how loved and precious we are in His sight. Before we were born, He had already paid the price for every sin we would ever commit. When we received Christ as Savior we were reconciled to God and made as righteous as He is. That is the truth about us, and He believes it and is declaring it even before we've opened our mouths to confess something we did. As believers, even when we fail, He calls us His beloved children, holy and dearly loved. That's how He wants us to speak life over others.

Even today, begin speaking words of life over yourself, your spouse, your children, your whole family, your friends, your co-workers, and everyone you can think of. Thank God for them. Call those things that be not as though they are. See it and say it. Even if you are having a difficult time with someone, that must not be the substance of your speech. Prophesy what is not yet seen with the natural eyes. I've been speaking life over my husband for nearly three decades. It's easy to do with him because so much of it is already visible in his life. However, I keep declaring words, such as: Tom is wise and blessed, he's a man of prayer and loves to read the Word, he's happy and prosperous in every area of life and generous with what he has, he's always filled with joy and kindness, he is healthy and full of energy. Tom stewards his time really well. Tom is romantic, spontaneous, and always fun to be with; he's a wonderful father and husband. Tom makes wise decisions and has Holy-Spirit-inspired initiatives. Far too many people criticize their spouses, even behind their backs, and it can be really destructive. That just makes matters worse. Declare not what you think you see with your eyes but what God envisions for everyone in your life. What sort of person do you want your spouse to be? See it and say it. These life-giving words empower our loved ones to be who God has called them to be.

> Prophesy what is not yet seen
> with the natural eyes.

God made sure Sarah did that with Abraham. His original name, Abram, meant "exalted father," but God changed his name to Abraham, which means "father of multitudes," as a prophecy of the promise He had given. I'm sure it wasn't easy for Sarah to keep calling her husband "father of multitudes" before they ever had a son, but that was the name God had given him. Can you imagine what that must have been like for her? They were both very elderly and in the natural considered barren, but she called Abraham by his God-given identity, and it opened the way for the promise to be realized.

BETWEEN ASKING AND RECEIVING

I love asking God for things. In fact, He says, *"You have not, because you ask not" (James 4:2, KJV)*. He invites us to ask and my list of requests is quite long. I love bringing them to Him because I know that when I ask, I receive. That's what He promises. However, there's something important that needs to happen in between the asking and receiving. We see a hint of it in Philippians 4:6–7, a great passage about asking God for what we need: *"Be anxious for nothing, but in everything by prayer and supplication, with thanksgiving, let your requests be made known to God; and the peace of God, which surpasses all understanding, will guard your hearts and minds through Christ Jesus."* That little phrase, "with thanksgiving," tells us we can go ahead and give thanks for what God is going to do, even though we haven't seen the answer yet. In His eyes, it's already an established fact; we just haven't gotten to it yet on our earthly time line. If that's true, then we can go ahead and count on it in our conversations with Him and in our internal self-talk and our words with others. You can be discreet about that. You will want to be sure it lines up with the word and character of God, and you probably won't want to state your bold declarations in front of people who would only think you're crazy for saying them. In your personal life and in your close relationships, go ahead and speak the truth, even when it hasn't come to pass yet.

I was praying for someone recently who had a health issue with his lungs, so I asked God to heal him. I asked that when he had the next scan, there would be no problem, no nodules, no tumors, no health issues at all. Then I thanked God for healing him, for making this next scan so clear that the doctors would be confused about it. I thanked Him until I actually felt the feelings of the answer, getting excited about what God was doing. My spirit did a little happy dance over it. But I knew I still had another weapon. I began speaking it out, declaring his healing, seeing his lungs as completely healthy and talking about them as though they were healed. That's how I pray because I believe there is so much more to it than just asking. Asking is very important, but so is believing, and our mouths speak what our hearts believe. Faith shows up in our gratitude, our emotions, and our words.

This emotional aspect of speaking life is important. As we've noted, this is not a ritual or a formula. Just saying certain words does not necessarily produce any particular effect. The difference comes when we really believe what we say and sense the weight or the joy of it; we can then speak with greater power. This is the same dynamic that is at work in many prophetic words in Scripture. In Isaiah, for example, God tells childless women to rejoice over their children: *"Sing, O barren, you who have not borne! Break forth into singing, and cry aloud, you who have not labored with child!" (Isaiah 54:1).* Telling childless women who long to get pregnant to rejoice might seem cruel if you don't realize what's behind it. God is urging them to actually get excited about what He is going to do. He wants us to be seeing the things we are declaring, speaking them out in faith, and rejoicing over the fulfillment. As you begin to operate like your Father, in calling things that are not as though they are, you begin believing them to the point that you experience the emotion and joy of having them already.

What does that look like? If, for example, you are praying for a loved one who is not yet saved, you stop talking about what you see. Don't complain about their attitude or their skeptical views. That just reinforces the lie. The more you judge them with your words and the more you declare those things you see in them, the more you build a wall that makes it difficult for them to come through. Instead, speak creatively in order to open up a way for them to come into God's presence. See them as God has called them to be. He has already revealed that it is not His will for anyone to perish, so you can know that you are praying and declaring His will for them to be saved. So ask Him what that looks like. Envision it. See what He is doing in them. See how they are so full of love, how they have completely reordered their priorities, how they are passionate about Jesus. In their true identities, they speak words of wisdom, demonstrate the kindness and compassion of God, and live with such integrity. Let your respect for them rise up within you. Thank God for the picture of what He is doing. As you begin to believe it, also begin to declare it. Then, whenever you do interact with them, you will find yourself filled with hope. Instead of encountering your judgment, they begin to sense a way that they might come into what you are seeing, even if they aren't aware of what it is. The more you call things that are not as though they are, the more you begin to see them in their true reality.

Do everything you can to avoid the common temptation that comes after we have made our requests of God. You will notice obstacles and contradictions to your answer. You will easily recognize the problem, but do not declare everything you see with your natural eyes or reasoning. Do not prophesy the problem. Prophesy the solution, the promise, the answer that is coming. Even as you speak it, hope begins to rise in your heart. Faith attaches to it, and you become a vessel for establishing God's will on earth.

I'm not suggesting that you live in denial. I am suggesting, however, that you speak from a sense of purpose. Instead of complaining about whatever is going on with a spouse's behavior, an illness or pain, a problem that doesn't seem to go away, start calling those things that be not as though they are. His Word does not return to Him void without accomplishing what it was sent forth to do. It is quick and it is powerful and you have the authority to send it forth. Speak it specifically and deliberately. Whatever you can see in your spirit and say with your mouth, you can have in your life. This is not a magic formula; it's a matter of getting a picture in your mind and speaking it out by faith. Declare that your life is getting sweeter and sweeter, that your family is falling more and more in love with God, that your children are walking in the power of the Lord. Fill in the blanks of your life with words of life, and you will eat the delicious fruit of God's blessings.

I get very sad when I hear couples speaking in destructive ways about each other. "My husband is so lazy . . ." "My wife always complains . . ." There are a lot of reasons you should never say anything so negative, but two of the biggest reasons are that it is very dishonoring and you are reinforcing what you don't like. Is that really what you want to see increasing in your life? Do you want more of the same? No, if you want things to change, speak change. Declare how generous, hardworking, loving, kind-hearted, patient, spiritually minded, and wise your spouse is. If you start speaking that way in your private time with the Lord, you actually open the door for your husband or wife to step into that reality. When you see him or her again, you will find yourself feeling less judgmental and demonstrating more respect. You begin to believe the best.

Tom and I make these kinds of confessions about each other and about other people all the time. We believe the best of people because God is love and love believes the best. If we are in Him, that's the kind of love we have. When we speak this way, it changes our mind-set. It takes us against the grain of our human culture, which is so focused on criticism and faultfinding. Our culture should be the culture of heaven. We make confessions about people that agree with heaven's conversation about them. Love is patient and kind, so I am patient and kind. That's what I want to create in the people around me.

The Bible says, *"The tongue has the power of life and death" (Proverbs 18:21, NIV)*. I wonder sometimes if people are aware of how their words can make others feel. I've heard casual comments about people's clothes, hair, makeup, blemishes, posture, expressions, voices, and other personal characteristics that may mean little to the speaker but wound the hearer's heart. Scripture counsels us to be careful with what we say. *"There is one who speaks like the piercings of a sword, but the tongue of the wise promotes health" (Proverbs 12:18)*. We have the power to heal or to wound. Paul elaborates on this in Ephesians when he urges his readers, *"Let no corrupt word proceed out of your mouth, but what is good for necessary edification, that it may impart grace to the hearers" (Ephesians 4:29)*. In other words, don't just say whatever comes to mind. Think to yourself, *Does this impart grace?* If not, don't say it! Your words should make people feel loved and accepted because that is God's heart toward them. Self-control is one of the fruits of the

Holy Spirit, and we all have to learn to control our mouths. Your tongue is a powerful weapon, a sharp sword that can wound people if you're not careful.

That can be really difficult to remember, when people are coming against you with criticism or unkind words themselves. It's easy to speak unkind words in return, and it feels appropriate. Remember, just because you feel like saying something it doesn't mean you have a good reason to say it. Some desires are not godly desires. Evaluate your words, choose to be constructive rather than destructive, to heal, and restore situations rather than make them worse. The truth, as you understand it, does not always need to be spoken. When it does, we need to be careful to speak the truth in love rather than just loving to speak the truth. There's a big difference. People who love to speak the truth can be a little scary, and they can wound people more deeply than they think.

I often tell a story about a prophecy I received years ago about the time I was starting to write songs. A well-meaning man pulled me aside and said, "I see a clock, and it's at quarter past the hour. I feel the Lord saying that your songwriting is one-quarter anointed and three-quarters unanointed." That was it. I went home thinking I didn't want to write any more songs.

If he had thought through that word a little bit and considered how it could be used to edify and impart grace, he could have said, "I think the clock represents your songwriting, and God wants to increase your anointing threefold." Same word, different delivery, and an entirely different effect. I would have gone home and picked up my pen.

I realize not everything is going to come out right, and some of us are better at arranging words than others. But if we think about these things and ask whether our words are likely to edify and impart grace, we will translate our good motives into good results. The power of the tongue can produce either despair or hope. It can lay a heavy weight on people's hearts or bring deliverance and freedom. A prophecy of Jesus says, *"A bruised reed He will not break"* *(Proverbs 42:3)*. Some people see a bruised reed and say, "Wow, you're really bruised." Then they just leave their words behind to create wounds. A fool blurts things out, but a wise man uses his tongue to bring health, life, wholeness, and healing.

A good guideline for speaking words that are good and necessary for edification and imparting grace, to the hearer, is in another passage that speaks about thinking the right thoughts. Philippians 4:8 says, *"Whatever things are true, whatever things are noble, whatever things are just, whatever things are pure, whatever things are lovely, whatever things are of good report, if there is any virtue and if there is anything praiseworthy, meditate on these things."* If we are meditating on those things, we are much more likely to speak these things because our words flow from our hearts and minds. This Scripture is a great checklist for filtering our words to build people up, give them hope, and speak creatively into their destinies. No matter how tempted you are to tell someone what you really think about them, think about whether your words will help them or keep them stuck where they are. Then go back and work on what you think about them. You cannot and should not determine your words based on natural appearances.

Very often when I'm prophesying in a meeting, the Holy Spirit will highlight someone in the back or on the edges. Often everyone else in the room is aware of their circumstances or background. Sometimes the messages I get for these people are the most wonderfully encouraging words, and I can almost sense people in the crowd thinking, *Why would someone like that get such a powerful word?* The answer is because they need a word like that. God wants to pull people into their destinies, and He does it by speaking things that are not as though they are. He wants to open the door of their understanding to recognize who they really are. They are not ugly ducklings, not misfits, not people who have blown it so badly they can never be restored. God gives hope, declares destiny, and assures us of His plans to prosper us, not to harm us, and to give us a hope and a future. Anyone can call out the state someone is currently in. That takes no prophetic insight at all. God wants to teach us another way and calls people out of their present state into their future destinies.

Some people seem to think that the way to call people into their destinies is to correct them. If you have a ministry of correction, I'd suggest taking a few weeks to meditate on that list of worthwhile thoughts in Philippians 4:8. It's followed by a promise that the God of peace will be with you, and if you allow it to shape your words, it will bring the hope and peace Jesus brought to people. You simply cannot continue to focus negatively on the issues of other people's lives. God has called us to think about higher thoughts that are noble, pure, holy, and praiseworthy. The world is highly intrigued with scandalous, unlovely stories containing sordid details, which explains the success of tabloids, talk shows, and criminal reports. Instead, we need to be fascinated with whatever is pure and praiseworthy. Why? Because out of the abundance of the heart, the mouth speaks. If you are fixated on whatever is noble and true, it will be much easier to agree with what God says about you when He gives you a noble and true report, and it will be much easier to speak those empowering words to others because you will have prepared your mind to believe them. If your mind is continually being drawn to that which is ugly and sinful, you will see the ugly and sinful behind every action and read impure motives into others' behaviors.

Think twice before you describe someone else. Your descriptions define people with words, and God does not want you to define anyone improperly. Speak life so freely that you become known by your love.

WORDS OF HONOR

I love being around people who never say an ugly word about someone else. That's rare in our culture, where it's normal to pull people down and rare to give compliments without qualifying them with a touch of criticism. When people haven't embraced the truth of what God feels about them, they feel frustrated, angry, envious, suspicious, and they subconsciously try to pull others down to their level. All of that goes away when you immerse yourself in what God says about you. You are holy, beloved, chosen, clothed with the kindness, humility and the patience of Jesus. All of the virtues of God are yours by faith. That frees you up to affirm others, encourage them, give compliments freely, and bless them with the truths of God. Your tongue is a powerful weapon for changing the world around you.

A simple word *"fitly spoken"* can be like an apple of gold in settings of silver *(Proverbs 25:11)*. It can be a gift that changes someone's day or even his or her life. *"Anxiety in the heart of man causes depression, but a good word makes it glad" (Proverbs 12:25)*. You can be that person who brings a kind word. When I talk to a shop attendant or a fellow customer, instead of making small talk about the weather or the news, I often find something kind to say. "You have beautiful eyes." "I love your smile." My daughter likes to watch the shop attendants because they don't always know what to do with a compliment like that. It shifts things. The atmosphere changes. You may not have an opportunity to share the gospel in situations like that, but you can still give someone an encounter with the kindness of God. Sometimes that's all it takes to start opening a heart to believe. At the very least, it demonstrates that (in spite of popular opinion) Christians aren't mean, judgmental people, but that maybe believers are loving after all. As Jesus said, that's how people will know we are His disciples, if we love one another.

Don't waste your words on worthless things. Let people know how loved and beautiful they are. Show them the Father's heart. Pointing out someone's kind disposition or warm smile might seem like a small thing to you, but it can have tremendous impact. I still remember kind words spoken to me when I was a child by people I loved and respected. I treasured the words of parents and teachers and still do. You have the opportunity to shape a child's heart with the kindness of God or to break off anxiety, heal wounds, and bring freedom to a stranger. All it takes is a moment. The results can last forever.

There's an old saying most of us were taught as children that says sticks and stones may break our bones, but words will never hurt us. I wish that were true, but it isn't. Words can hurt far worse than sticks and stones. They can stay with us for a lifetime, if we accept them and let them sink in. Some people go through a lifetime of difficult circumstances without ever hearing kind words spoken to them personally. Some have been pierced so often by sharp words and are so emotionally scarred that they hardly know how to be encouraged. What if your kind word today was treasured in someone's heart for a lifetime? As believers who are overflowing with the goodness of God and have drunk deeply from the river of His pleasure over us, we have more than enough kindness to give away.

Ask God for wisdom and words. Thank Him for His extravagant mercy, for bathing you in His love, for showing you what it means to be deeply adored and treasured. Get filled up with His goodness so fully and freely that you overflow with it. You carry the fragrance of Christ wherever you go. Use your words to enrich the lives around you. They will open hearts and draw people into the family of God.

DECLARATIONS
FOR OTHERS

The declarations listed in the last chapter for yourself can also apply to other people. All of the following are taken from a biblical basis and can be prayed for and believed for on behalf of other people, calling those things that be not as though they are with a confidence that it is the will of God:

- The fervent prayer of a righteous person accomplishes much. I have been made righteous; therefore, my prayers for people are powerful and effective (James 5:16; Romans 5:1).

- My family is saved (Acts 16:31).

- God will contend with those who contend with me and will rescue and deliver my children (Isaiah 49:25).

- The Father is drawing the people I pray for closer to Jesus (John 6:44).

- God is giving them a spirit of wisdom and revelation in the knowledge of Him (Ephesians 1:17).

- They will know the hope of His calling, the riches of His inheritance, and His power toward those who believe (Ephesians 1:18–19).

- They are being rooted and grounded in every dimension of Jesus' love in order to be filled with the fullness of God (Ephesians 3:17–19).

- They will know God's will and walk in a manner worthy of Him, pleasing to Him, fruitful in His work (Colossians 1:9–10).

- They are being strengthened with His power for all endurance and patience with joy (Colossians 1:11).

- The God of hope will fill them with joy and peace by faith (Romans 15:13).

- They will prosper and be in health, just as their soul prospers (3 John 2).

- I have the calling and the authority to forgive sins in Jesus' name (John 20:23).

- I have the calling and the authority to bless people with God's favor and His shining face, His grace in their lives, and the fullness of His peace in their hearts (Numbers 6:24–26).

5

SPEAK LIFE OVER CIRCUMSTANCES

REORDERING YOUR WORLD

Sheri was going through a difficult time. She and her husband were both Christians and had brought up their children in the faith. As a result of some bad financial decisions made by her husband, they had lost everything and went through a series of relational crises that led first to a separation and then a divorce. This also affected her son who was not on speaking terms with his mother for months. Sheri was desperate, and she began fasting and praying fervently for God to intervene in her family. She had always considered herself to be a generally positive person, but after hearing my message on the power of words, she recalled a lot of things she wished she hadn't said. She began to repent for comments that had been critical of her husband during their financial difficulties, for focusing on the problems they were facing and not on God's solutions, for not encouraging and supporting him and for not creating the kind of verbal environment that brings the kingdom to earth.

God had already done a lot in response to Sheri's fasting and praying. After about a week, the son who had not spoken to her in six months, texted and wanted to talk. They reunited. After another week, another son who had never applied for a job and had few visible prospects suddenly got a great job in information technology. But when Sheri heard this message on speaking life and realized how often she had not done so, she spent two days crying and resolving to change the way she spoke. She talked to her ex-husband and asked for his forgiveness for not supporting him and for speaking critically and destructively. Soon after, they began dating again.

Sheri's words created a new environment in their relationship and love began to grow again. Now, after five years of separation, they are planning to remarry!

I was so blessed to hear Sheri's testimony because it so clearly reveals that we are not just the victims of our circumstances. We have a right and an opportunity to step into the inheritance God has for us and to steward it well. At any point, we can pick up the weapons of our warfare, which are mighty for the pulling down of strongholds, and begin speaking life. And when we do, things change. Sometimes they change right away, as they did with Sheri, and sometimes they take more time. But sooner or later, our circumstances will always bend to the creative force of our faith-filled words.

What are you saying about your circumstances? Are you focusing on the problems in your conversations or are you speaking positively and creatively about solutions? Do your words reinforce what's wrong or create what's right? If you aren't really careful, you may find that in spite of your best intentions, you are entrenching the very things you don't want in your world with your words.

One of the ways we tend to categorize people is by their optimism. Do they see the glass as half empty or half full? The truth is that most of us, even the optimists among us, have a natural tendency to zoom in on whatever is going wrong in our lives and try to fix it. The glass can be 98 percent full, but we think it's the 2 percent left over that needs our full attention. Psychologists talk about something called "negativity bias" that skews our focus toward problems. It's the thought process that commands our attention when a child brings home a report card with six A's and one C, or that highlights one negative comment amidst a hundred positive ones after a project or performance is completed, or that makes it easier to believe a negative outcome in a situation instead of all the possible positive ones. It's the tendency to notice everything that is lacking, out of line, in disrepair, and in need of a solution.

The problem with being problem focused is that we end up filling our minds with the small percentage of "wrong" in our lives and neglect the high percentage of "right." When a health issue comes up, our first response is not usually to thank God for everything that is working well; it's to think in crisis terms about what could be wrong. We take a God-given awareness of problems and get stuck there, and it really skews our perspective. It undermines gratitude and creates anxiety, which can turn to depression, and worst of all, it actually magnifies the problem because whatever we focus on gets larger in our own minds and very often in actual circumstances.

I know a couple who recently identified this dynamic in their conversations and resolved never to discuss a problem unless the primary focus of their words was on the solution. They would focus on what God was doing in the situation, what He might do, or how He might want them to respond to it in faith. It does no one any good to identify a problem, describe how bad it is, and leave it sitting there. That only makes it worse. It also makes life depressing and strains relationships. What God would have us do when we see a problem is thank Him for everything that is going right, thank Him that He already has a solution for the problem, and then ask Him how He might want us to participate in the solution. Our words surrounding that issue need to be positive, hopeful, and full of expectation and faith. Why?

Because that's how God sees it. There is no problem out there for which He is at a loss, wondering what to do or desperately hoping it works out well. When that perspective fills our minds, we are out of sync with Him. He already has a solution, and it will be glorious. That is the perspective that needs to shape our thoughts and our words.

This is both a deep spiritual truth and basic psychology. When a golfer focuses on the next shot thinking, *Don't slice it, don't slice it, whatever you do, don't slice it*, can you guess what is likely to happen? When a goal kicker thinks, *Don't miss this attempt, don't miss the angle, don't embarrass yourself*, what do you think the likely outcome will be? Those situations rarely work out well because their thoughts simply reinforce the negative possibilities. Our focus very often becomes our reality. Instead, athletes are trained to visualize things working out perfectly (the perfect shot, the next score, the right strategy). That is not only good psychology it is a biblical principle. When we focus on answers, solutions, favor, and blessing, that's what we tend to experience.

*Our focus very often
becomes our reality.*

God created the world with words, declaring what would be when it did not yet exist. We have seen how that same God created us with the same anointing on our lives to speak and create. Death and life are in the power of the tongue, and we have the choice about how we're going to use that power. He gives us amazing promises about declaring truth, about speaking to mountains in order to move them. These promises are not just for those who are "super-spiritual" but for everyone who believes. He has created us to be "prophetic solutionists" who see the problem for what it is (just for a moment), but then dwell on the solutions He has for it. When we recognize that potential and put it into practice, He does exceedingly, abundantly beyond all that we can ask or imagine.

I know the difference this can make. I have seen it in countless lives like Sheri's and in my own experience. Not long ago, a particular conference came to mind, and I told the Lord, "I'd really like to speak at that one." It was just a random little thought, but I said it out loud to Tom. "I'm going to speak at that conference." And then a few months later, the invitation came. It was like a kiss from God reaffirming that yes, you can actually have what you say. I really believe God is looking for us to step into the fullness of what He has for us. He wants us to bring Him the desires of our hearts and say, "Lord, this is what I'm sensing. Does it line up with Your Word and Your character?" If His answer is yes, then we need to recognize that desire as a divine invitation waiting for our response. And our response is simply to see it, believe it, and say it.

BE ANXIOUS FOR NOTHING

Your own anxieties will go to battle against any response of faith. Your inner dialogue can be filled with fear. If you aren't very careful, worry will set up camp in your mind and sap you of strength. That internal conversation is actually feeding poison to your soul. Even when you know better, even when you tell yourself that you shouldn't be worried about it and try to have faith instead, the voice still comes. It still ticks away in the background.

We have looked at Philippians 4:6–7 a couple of times already, but it is especially relevant to asking, declaring, and receiving God's will for your circumstances.

> *Be anxious for nothing, but in everything by prayer and supplication, with thanksgiving, let your requests be made known to God; and the peace of God, which surpasses all understanding, will guard your hearts and minds through Christ Jesus. (Philippians 4:6–7)*

This Scripture begins with an acknowledgment that our circumstances actually do cause anxiety in us. Otherwise, Paul would not have instructed the Philippians not to be anxious. Instead of worrying about the situations we face, we can bring our requests to God, with the very important attitude of thanksgiving and know that He will handle them well. We can be so confident in His answers, that our hearts go ahead and rest peacefully in the knowledge that He is working things out. He would not tell us to be anxious for nothing if things were still up in the air or if He knew the outcome would devastate us. He says to be anxious for nothing because when we have given Him our requests with gratitude, there is actually nothing to be anxious about. Our hearts can be at peace.

If you want a picture of what that looks like, here's how I follow the instructions of that verse in my prayers. I make my requests (I've mentioned that I usually have a long list of them, and God doesn't mind at all because He invites us to ask) and talk to Him about each of those things. I ask Him what His will is, whether it lines up with His Word and His ways, and to show me His perspective on things so I'll know I'm praying in unison with the conversation in heaven. Then when I've asked, I begin to thank God for what He has already done, what He is doing now, and what He is going to do in the situation. I start confessing and declaring the truth of what I've been asking about. I may declare something like this: "Thank You, Father, that I have everything I need, that You are providing more than enough to accomplish Your will and answer these prayers. Thank You that this meeting will be financed, that thousands are being saved, that people are being healed, and that work is being done with excellence. Thank You that doors are opening and closing according to Your purposes, and the right doors will open at the right time, just as You have planned.

Thank You that no problem or illness or obstacle can stand against You. You've got this covered. I am so, so grateful." Whether the circumstance you are praying about is financial, professional, relational, physical, emotional, academic, ministry oriented, or anything else, He has already made a way, and you can express your gratitude for what He has already purposed to do. In many cases, God has already begun working. He has answers ready before we even pray. Go ahead and thank Him for those.

If I'm asking for finances, I start declaring the provision as though it has already come. If I'm asking for opportunities, I start envisioning doors opening and declare them opened. If I'm thinking about a health issue for someone, I'll start praising God for that person's health. Like the barren woman who sings (Isaiah 54:1), I'll go ahead and get happy about the answer and sing some hallelujahs. I'll cheer, dance, and shout "hooray" and "hallelujah," or whatever else I feel about the answer being on its way. It becomes real to me, even when I haven't seen it physically. I envision the doctors' good reports, the checks with lots of zeros, the invitation emails, or whatever is relevant to the situation. I want it to become a "done deal" in my mind. The important thing in addition to calling those things that are not as though they are is knowing that they really are. That's faith and it is the currency of God's kingdom. That's how His promises are fulfilled and His answers come.

Remember, you are not trying to talk yourself into something that isn't real. You are talking yourself out of something that isn't God's promised reality, to transform your old false perceptions into new, true ones. This is not a mind game; it is a matter of stepping into the realities that God has promised for us. His desire is for us to have abundant life. Jesus said so (John 10:10). His will is for us to prosper and be in health even as our soul prospers (3 John 1:2). He wants us to fully experience the righteousness, peace, and joy of the kingdom through the Holy Spirit (Romans 14:17). He wants to give us hope and a future (Jeremiah 29:11), to bless us, make His face shine on us, and be gracious to us (Numbers 6:25). The blessings could go on and on (you'll find a lot more listed at the end of this book), but it is important to know that these are God's will for you. You don't have to add "if it's Your will" to your prayers for these things. He has already revealed that they are. You have no need to be anxious for *anything*. You are a son or daughter of the King who has the power to bring the kingdom into existence with your words.

I had a dream in which I was walking and talking with a tall man with dark hair. I had never seen him before, yet he also seemed familiar to me. Somehow I knew he was my senior pastor. We were having a conversation, and I asked him, "What do you think about this person for that position?"

"That's a really good idea," he said. "I think that would work very well." Then he asked if I'd considered another person for a different position.

"That's an awesome idea," I answered. "Yes, let's do that."

The conversation went on like that for a little while, each of us bringing up ideas and getting the other's opinion. Then I woke up feeling wonderful about the dream. The Holy Spirit spoke to me: "I'm your Senior Pastor." I realized that I don't have to figure everything out. I'm not walking through life on my own. I can lean on Him in any situation. I thought through the conversation we'd had in the dream and noticed He had never given a command. This was not a conversation about moral imperatives; He was coaching me through decisions I needed to make. I might have expected God to say, "You must do this" and "Thou shalt do that," as if everything coming from Him must be followed by a "thus saith the Lord." That's not what the Father is like. A good father doesn't treat a child who is growing up and starting to take responsibility as someone who needs to be controlled. He encourages, empowers, and helps us make decisions that fit with His purposes and His character. It would be quite out of character for Him to say, "I've given you the mind of Christ and the wisdom of the Holy Spirit, but I don't trust you to make any decisions on your own. Just listen to My command." There are times when He tells us exactly what to do, of course, but more often He leads us and helps us grow in our decision-making. He thinks we have the capacity to make amazing, wonderful decisions and has actually equipped us to do so. He doesn't want to be a dictator. He wants to draw out what He has put into us.

Remember this when you are worrying about something and letting your anxiety get the best of you. The Father wants you to begin to access the Holy Spirit so you don't have to be anxious. You don't need to worry about how things are going to happen or whether you are making exactly the right decision.

Talk to Him about it, and He will guide you. If you make an honest mistake and get a little off course, He will steer you back on to it. Do everything in conversation with Him, and you really will be able to be anxious for nothing.

Free from anxiety, then, you can simply thank Him for what He has done, is doing, and will do in the future. Envision the reality of His will for you. "Thank You, Lord, that all things are possible for those who believe. Thank You that I have nothing to worry about, that I walk in ever-increasing health, that my house is paid off, that I have provision for every need, that my children are faithfully walking in their destinies, that You delight in me and I delight in You, and that You are giving me the desires of my heart." Whether you see these things yet in the natural realm is not the issue; you are learning to see them in the spiritual realm. You speak from that vision and things happen.

THE FRUIT OF YOUR WORDS

Years ago, I developed some nodules on my vocal chords from preaching, leading worship, and ministering at the altar over loud music. My voice was scratchy, and I lost all of my singing range. I had to get other people to preach and lead worship. While in some ways it was good to learn to delegate and let other people grow in their gifts and responsibilities, I knew it was not God's will for me to be sick. I was told I needed to see an expensive speech therapist every week, even though I had been trained as a speech and drama teacher and knew that I should be warming up my voice before using it and being careful not to strain my voice. Unfortunately, because I had been careless, the damage had already been done, and I was told I would probably have to have an operation. It was all very discouraging.

Then the Lord challenged me to speak life over these depressing circumstances. So I would get up in the morning with my throat hurting, and in my very scratchy voice, I would struggle to say, "My voice is strong and clear, and I can sing beautifully. I have a great vocal range. I can reach high notes and low notes." Again and again, every day, I would repeat the same phrases over and over again, with my voice sounding exactly the opposite of what I was declaring. Nothing happened for a while. However, after three months, all of a sudden, everything came back to normal. I had my full range again, I could speak in a strong and clear voice, and everything was fine. I didn't need the operation I was told would be necessary. God completely healed me.

I learned something in that process: that we need to choose whether we are going to sit back and be victims or whether we are going to get up and do something about our circumstances. Even when there is nothing we can do in the natural, visible world, there is something we can do in the invisible realm. The weapons of our warfare are not carnal but are mighty in God for the pulling down of strongholds. We have been given a very powerful tool called a tongue. Just as God's Word is like a two-edged sword that can cut both ways, so are the words of those made in His image. When we come into agreement with God and begin to speak life, we are healed. Circumstances change. We have a choice to either sit back and be miserable or to speak up and be overcomers. I've done both. I can promise you; pity parties are never as satisfying as the enemy makes them out to be. We get much more fulfillment out of speaking life.

You really can eat the fruit of your words. We have looked at several proverbs that tell us about the power of words, two of which assure us that death and life are in the power of the tongue and that we will be satisfied with the fruit of our mouths (Proverbs 18:20–21). Again and again, Scripture reaffirms this. We can create the world around us with our words. Grumbling and complaining create an awful environment and produce very unsatisfying fruit, whilst words of light and life bring blessing after blessing. We get to choose.

THE FRUIT OF FAITH

Everything we do in the kingdom is by faith. You can have all of God's blessings and walk in His favor daily, but only by faith. If you don't apply faith to your circumstances, the promises of God sit on the shelf and you go your way without them. If you want to live a life of power, walking in the fruit of the Holy Spirit and the good works God has prepared for you, you will need to be deliberate about making declarations. A lot of people hope and wish for these things without actually applying their faith. God says you already have the power you need. He has already declared His "yes" and "amen" to all of His promises in Christ. Why not go ahead and ask, see the answer, declare it again and again, and expect to receive it? I have to be reminded constantly of this too. Sometimes I surprise myself when I realize all

I've done is made my requests in quiet prayer. The Holy Spirit has to prompt me: "Why don't you speak it out? Why don't you thank me for it? Why don't you declare it as though it is already happening?" Afterward, I think, *Oh that's right. I know that. I really should do that.* I have to apply the wisdom I've already been given. If you want to receive answers as the fruit of your faith, you need to do this too.

You may have noticed that a lot of what we have covered so far is really about the distinction between hoping something happens and actually believing that God has already answered you. When you really believe, you can go ahead and give thanks, declare what you know, and get happy about the reality of it. God wants us to come to the place where we're so excited about what He's going to do that we sing and dance, get genuinely thankful, and have peace and joy in our hearts. You can then celebrate the promise even before you have seen it in the natural. He wants our words and emotions to be paired with our faith so that the fruit of it actually comes. No matter how ridiculous that might seem to some and how foolish we appear when we behave this way, it works—over and over again.

Don't let your threatening circumstances unsettle you. If you have a medical test coming up, don't let your thoughts run along the natural course: "Oh, God, please, let it be okay. I hope it's all right. Please, Lord." You can bring the concern to Him, picture the results being clear, line up your declarations with the picture you have seen, and let your emotions get excited about the outcome. Even for the seemingly minor issues in your life, go ahead and deal with worrisome thoughts in the same way. Take captive those concerns that sap your strength even when they are still hiding in the background. That's what I do every morning. I take a mental inventory of my major and minor thoughts to see what I'm really concerned about. When something comes up, I talk to the Father about it. I bring the weight of it to Him and thank Him that I don't have to deal with anything on my own. I look through my journals to see if the concern is something He has already spoken to me about. Sometimes I discover that He has given me a really encouraging word, and I know it still applies. His words don't have an expiration date. Sometimes it's a new issue and He gives me fresh wisdom. Either way, I speak out what He has told me, then I go to the next concern and go through the same process. I thank Him for the wisdom I've already received and the wisdom He is going to give me. I thank Him that I will make a great decision about whatever circumstances I'm facing. I don't have to let all these little worries drain me of energy all day long. The Bible says it's *"The little foxes that spoil the vine" (Song of Solomon 2:15)*. I actively see what I'm believing, I say it out loud, and I praise God with joy in my heart. Eventually, I walk through the doors that have opened.

ENVISION YOUR DAY, CREATE YOUR WORLD

You don't need to wait until worries come to start speaking life. You can be proactive about envisioning and speaking creatively about your circumstances. I once read that William Branham used to ask God what was going to happen in his healing services before he walked into them. The Lord would show him different people who needed healing. In his spirit, he would see what their ailments looked like and how the Lord wanted to heal them. He would then go into the meetings and experience what he had already seen. When I read that, I thought it was a great idea. I wanted to do that too.

The first time I tried was before one of our church's regular Friday night meetings. "Lord, You're no respecter of persons. You did this for William Branham; do it for me too. Show me what You're going to do tonight. Who are You going to heal?" In my mind, I saw a lady who had one leg shorter than the other. "How do You want to heal her?" I asked. I saw myself praying for her. She got slain in the Spirit, I got down on the floor with her and put my hand on her ankle, her ankle grew out, and I was so happy. This all happened before I even left the house to go to the meeting. That night, I gave a word of knowledge about someone with one leg shorter than the other (since I was new at this, I just said "someone here," instead of specifically saying a lady). I described how it was affecting the way this person walked. A lady came out of the seats and toward the front. She was wearing a dress like the one I had seen in my vision. I was so excited because I already knew what to do next. I laid hands on her, she fell to the ground, I got down with her and put my hand on her ankle, and her leg grew out. She jumped up and ran around the building saying, "I've never been able to do this!" It was so cool! We all celebrated. And I went home thinking, *I wonder why I don't do this more often.*

I began to ask God about more things and about the events of each day. "What do You want to do today, Lord?" Then I would start to picture the day and see it come to pass. I realized I could have been doing this all along, but I had never taken the time to stop, see, and declare. I just rushed off into my day. But there are invitations waiting for us, for anyone who will pick them up and use them. I began to make shifts in my daily routine, like not taking any appointments before 10:30 in the morning because I need time to pray, see, and declare things for the day. Often it doesn't even require a prophetic vision; we already know so much of the will of God through His Word. We know He wants us to be healed, so we can picture that every single day. We already know He wants people to be drawn to Him, to know and love Him deeply, so we can picture our family members, our friends and co-workers, anyone we know and declare what we know is God's will for them. We can envision God at work in our workplace or our church and ask Him what that looks like. When He shows us, we can immerse ourselves in that vision and speak it forth. Instead of just longing for things to happen, begin to see them and say them. Then they will begin to change.

This is so much better than complaining about the way things are. I've heard people complaining about their churches: "I don't really like our worship music." "Our leadership isn't making great decisions." "I don't agree with the direction this place is taking." Those kinds of comments aren't helping anyone. They don't add anything to the conversation. They don't create anything good. Why not make some declarations, not simply about what you want to see happen but what God might want to do there? Say things like, "The worship in our church is so glorious! People get caught up in the Holy Spirit's movements! The leaders are so engaged! People are being saved, transformed, and healed in the middle of worship!" Do you see the difference? We are not called to be critical consumers who complain about whatever is wrong. We are called to be overcomers who create whatever is good.

I get really specific with this sometimes. I think of appointments that are scheduled for the day and envision what they are going to be like. What attitude will I have? What needs are the other people bringing into it? How can I minister to their hearts? I imagine myself smiling, full of love and compassion, listening really well and expressing the compassion of Jesus.

I imagine what it will be like for people when they shake my hand, when I smile and say hello. I imagine being the aroma of Christ to those who are perishing, having favor with them so they open their hearts and receive His love. If I don't picture the events of the day, I'll just wander through them and hopefully respond well to the way they go. If I envision how they will go, I have more influence over the outcome. I've been given the life of Christ, and I want to be intentional with the gift. I want to steward Him well.

If you have been born again, it is no longer you who lives, but Christ who lives in you. You are not just an observer in this world. You are no longer a victim. You are not called to be a complainer. Jesus is not at work within you to wring His hands, worry about how things are going to work out, or speak negatively about people and circumstances. He is at work within you to bring His kingdom to earth. As we begin to realize who He is and who we are in Him, we will begin to think, speak, and behave differently. We will walk in victory and power.

Elisha asked for a double portion of Elijah's anointing. When Elijah was taken up into heaven and his mantle fell, Elisha picked it up and struck the river with it and the water parted. We have been given something even more powerful: the mantle of Jesus. He told us we would do *"greater works"* than He did *(John 14:12)*. We are not orphans on the outside of God's family looking for a way into the inner circle. We have been brought into the inner circle already, and Jesus' power is in our hands. We can speak His words and see them come to pass.

DECLARATIONS
FOR YOUR CIRCUMSTANCES

As with the lists in previous chapters, these declarations are just the beginning. Explore what God has done in Scripture and see every miracle, every provision, every answered prayer as an invitation for you to ask Him to do the same.

- All things work out for my good (Romans 8:28).

- God provides all of my needs according to His riches in Glory (Philippians 4:19).

- Nothing is impossible for me because I am a believer (Mark 9:23).

- No weapon formed against me prospers (Isaiah 54:17).

- God opens doors of opportunity in my life and closes doors that should not be open to me (Revelation 3:7).

- God sets a table for me in the presence of my enemies (Psalm 23:5).

- God always brings me through in triumph (Isaiah 43:2).

- God is directing my path (Proverbs 3:5–6).

- I am receiving double blessing for all the trouble I've experienced (Isaiah 61:7).

- God is my very present help in any kind of trouble (Psalm 46:1).

- I am the head and not the tail. I am above and not beneath. I am not a victim of my circumstances; I overcome them (Deuteronomy 28:13).

- God does not withhold anything good from me (Psalm 84:11; Romans 8:32).

- I have mountain-moving faith (Mark 11:23).

- I am more than a conqueror in Jesus (Romans 8:37).

- God is stirred to action on my behalf and delivers me from my enemies (Psalm 18).

- God is making a way for me where there seems to be no way (Isaiah 43:16, 19; Romans 8:31).

- God is my strength and my deliverer, my fortress and my shield (Psalm 18:1–2).

- I have power to ascend the heights (Psalm 18:33; Habakkuk 3:19).

- God always leads me in triumph and spreads the fragrance of Jesus through me (2 Corinthians 2:14).

6

WALKING IN TRIUMPH

ON EARTH AS IT IS IN HEAVEN

David went through some seriously difficult situations for quite a long time. He had been rejected by King Saul, hunted continuously for years, slandered, and then rejected even by the Philistines. He had hidden out in caves, narrowly escaped death on several occasions, and endured all sorts of battles and hardships with his mighty men, who risked their lives to support him. One of the worst moments was when he and his men returned to their base camp at Ziklag after being sent away by the Philistines. They discovered that their camp had been raided and burned by Amalekites, and their wives and children had been taken captive. David and his men were stricken with grief, and even though his men had supported him through all the tumultuous years of his exile, they turned on him. The victories they had hoped for had not materialized. They knew that if David had taken advantage of two previous opportunities to kill Saul, they could have returned home much earlier, but David's sense of integrity had "wasted" those chances. These men had finally lost hope. They wanted to stone David.

That's a rough day. David's best friends wanted to kill him. David's wives and the wives and children of all his men were being held captive by ruthless enemies. Yet, even though David was greatly distressed, he did not give in to discouragement. In fact, the Bible says he strengthened himself in the Lord (1 Samuel 30:6).

Many of David's psalms follow the same trajectory. They begin in conflict and stress but end with declarations of hope and worship. One of my favorites is Psalm 27, which in its first few verses speaks of the wicked coming against David and an army encamping around him. But even before that, David declares the Lord to be his light and salvation and asks, *"Whom shall I fear?" (Psalm 27:1)*. David wasn't just being dramatic. He had good reason to be afraid; people were actually trying to kill him. Even in the midst of real concerns and probably even some fear, he did not allow himself to fall into despair, discouragement, or depression. He made a choice to say, "I know the will of my Father. I know God will cause me to triumph." As in the case of this psalm, *"Though an army may encamp against me, my heart shall not fear; though war may rise against me, in this I will be confident" (Psalm 27:3)*. David's focus was not on his fear or the problems he was facing; it was on God. His greatest desire was to dwell in the house of the Lord all the days of his life and behold the beauty of the Lord in His temple (Psalm 27:4). That temple would not be built on earth until the next generation, but David was gazing at the Lord and inquiring at a heavenly temple even more real than the earthly one. So David made his declarations from that place of worship: *"Now my head shall be lifted up above my enemies all around me; therefore I will offer sacrifices of joy in His tabernacle; I will sing, yes, I will sing praises to the Lord" (Psalm 27:6)*. Over the next few verses, he offers up his list of requests to God, making more declarations in the midst of them: *"When my father and my mother forsake me, then the Lord will take care of me" (Psalm 27:10).* In other words, even if the people who had been closest to him and were supposed to be his greatest support were to turn against him, God would still take care of him. Then finally, one of my favorites is verse 13: *"I would have lost heart, unless I had believed that I would see the goodness of the Lord in the land of the living."*

This is the confidence that comes out of a relationship with the One who wants you to triumph. When you know and believe that God is for you, when you come to Him every day and allow Him to reveal the deep, rich love He has for you, only then does your heart becomes confident. God doesn't expect you to trust someone you don't know. The more time you take to know Him, love Him, and receive His love, the more you find His perfect love casting out fear and deepening your roots in Him. Whenever hardship comes, whenever the enemy intimidates, whenever circumstances threaten, you are not moved because your roots go down deep into His love. Like David, you can say, "I will not fear even when an enemy encamps around me, even when everyone deserts me. I will not be afraid." Like Paul, you can declare, "If God is for me, who can be against me?" You live with a holy confidence and you do not lose heart. David had been through a long journey with a lot of trials and this psalm was written before he had seen the resolution of them all. He said he would have lost heart if he had not been convinced that he would see the goodness of the Lord not just one day in heaven but here on earth, in the land of the living. He believed what he had discovered and knew to be true and because of his belief, he declared it with confidence.

VICTORY: GOD'S WILL FOR YOUR LIFE

This is the confidence we should all be able to live with, that victory is God's will for our lives. Paul wrote about this victory in very certain terms:

Thanks be to God who always leads us in triumph in Christ, and through us diffuses the fragrance of His knowledge in every place. For we are to God the fragrance of Christ among those who are being saved and among those who are perishing. (2 Corinthians 2:14–15, TPT)

According to this verse, God always leads us in triumph in Christ. That's His will for us. We don't have to question whether God wants us to have victory; He manifests the aroma of Jesus through us so that others might know Him. We have seen in Romans 8 how the Holy Spirit and Jesus are interceding through us and for us in perfect harmony with the will of God. It says that Jesus is *"continually praying for our triumph" (Romans 8:34, TPT)*. That changes how we pray, doesn't it? We can no longer have an image of Jesus begging the Father to do something He wasn't planning to do or trying to twist the Father's arm on our behalf. He already knows what the Father wants to do and is talking to Him about it. He knows the Father wants us to triumph, to overcome, to prosper in all our endeavors, to walk in health, wisdom, love, and purity. The will of God is to manifest His life and victory in us and through us, so that we experience being the head and not the tail, above and not beneath. All through Scripture, we see that the will of God is for us to triumph.

That not only changes how I pray; it changes how I look at circumstances. As previously mentioned, F. F. Bosworth used to say that, "faith begins where the will of God is known." I can be confident that the will of God is not for our harm or continuing hardship. His will is for us to overcome and live in victory. Jesus is not interceding for us by asking the Father to teach us a good lesson by giving us a little more suffering or making us hang on a little longer so our faith can be strengthened. No, Jesus is for us. He is declaring, "Father, thank You that You have destined them always to overcome. Thank You that You are always leading them in triumph. Thank You for laying up good works in advance for them to do, that no weapon formed against them will ever prosper. Yes, Lord, open their eyes to see it and their hearts to receive it, to pull on the promises We have made for them." I believe that's what the prayer in heaven looks like.

We have been given the keys of the kingdom here on earth and whatever we bind on earth will have been bound in heaven and whatever we loose on earth will have been loosed in heaven (Matthew 18:18). Once we recognize the will of the Father and understand the declarations and prayers that are being made on our behalf in heaven, then we can play our part. We take the keys of the kingdom, the authority we have been given, and open up the gates of our hearts in expectation, saying, "Your will be done in my life and in my circumstances as it is in heaven!" In heaven, His will is being declared and decreed for our continual triumph. So we align our words with those declarations and decrees.

If you are not walking in continual triumph, then, it is not because your triumph isn't the will of God. It's because God wants you to step further in, to pray and declare, to open up the gates and begin to release on earth the will of the Father as it is in heaven. Come into agreement with Him and do not give up! We enter into the promises of God by faith and patience (Hebrews 6:13). His promise, for us, is to walk in victory.

We are not little orphans pleading for a crumb from the Father's table every once in a while. We have been invited into the family of God. We are children of the royal family and heirs of the kingdom estate. In fact, we are so close to Him that Jesus calls us His body. So you can be closer to God than you are to any person on earth. He will not deny you because He cannot deny His own flesh. He is for you.

HOLY OPTIMISM

God wants you to know and remember that it is His will for you to triumph continually. The Holy Spirit wants to release a holy, divine optimism in you that thinks, by default, "This is going to work out well." I know this because I've experienced, again and again, a shift that only He could inspire in the midst of disheartening situations. There have been times when I've been genuinely afraid. Fear is a normal human emotion, and it is not sinful to feel it. But when you feel fear, it is not God's will for your heart to yield to it. You do not have to be afraid. God wants you to know that He is faithful. He gives you revelation that you are going to see His goodness in the land of the living. He promises to work all things together for your good because you love Him and are called according to His purpose. He fills you with His Spirit, who will never inspire fear in you, no matter your circumstances. You can live with His holy optimism that is completely confident in every situation, that one way or another, both from an eternal perspective and at ground level, it will turn out well.

The more you declare His promises over your life, the more your faith in them increases. Your spirit listens to the sound of your own voice, so even when you don't feel the significance of what you're saying, you begin to align with it anyway. I say these things over myself all the time. "This is going to work out for my good because He said all things work together for the good of those who love Him and are called according to His purpose. That's me. Therefore, all things are working together for my good. This is going to turn out wonderfully. Lord, You said that for my former shame, pain, and disgrace, You would give me double recompense, so thank You that what the enemy is now trying to do will work out twice as good for me. I'm sowing this disappointment by faith so I can receive double blessing. Thank You for supernatural favor!" Even if I don't understand His plan yet or know all the answers at the moment, I get a great sense of joy that I'm not doing life on my own. I have full trust that God is completely on top of things. It's going to go well. This is not just positive thinking (although if the Bible says positive things about you, you really ought to agree with them). This is the Word of God based on knowledge of who He is.

You can live with His holy optimism that is completely confident in every situation.

FEAR, FAITH, AND THE AUTHORITY OF GOD

One day after ministering to multitudes by the Sea of Galilee, Jesus told His disciples, *"Let us cross over to the other side" (Mark 4:35)*. So they left the multitude, got into a boat, and headed across the lake. A violent storm came up, and waves were crashing into the boat. Somehow, Jesus remained asleep in the back, and the disciples could hardly believe He wasn't jumping into action. *"Teacher, do You not care that we are perishing?"* they pleaded. So Jesus got up, rebuked the wind, and said to the sea, *"Peace, be still!"* The wind stopped, the waves calmed down, and the disciples were amazed. Instead of Jesus saying, "Relax, you've got Me with you," He turned the responsibility back on them. *"Why are you so fearful? How is it that you have no faith?" (Mark 4:35–41)*.

This is such an interesting story. Jesus sensed God leading Him to the other side. The Holy Spirit was revealing the Father's will for Him to preach to Gentiles. That was Jesus' desire, and God gives us the desires of our hearts. He uses them for our direction. So, for example, you can know your desire to be healed is the will of God. It's in the Bible. God tells us that by Jesus' stripes, we are healed (Isaiah 53:5). He says not to forget all His benefits, and the first two benefits that psalm lists are forgiveness and healing (Psalm 103:2–3). Every single person who came to Jesus for healing was healed. He didn't turn any away, and He's the same yesterday, today, and forever.

Just like Jesus, you might run into a storm on your way to the other side. The fulfillment of your desire might seem to be blocked by an obstacle, something that causes fear and panic, if you aren't careful. *"Many are the afflictions of the righteous, but the Lord delivers him out of them all" (Psalm 34:19).* You may be righteous but suddenly get bad news about your health. You may run into unexpected, difficult circumstances. Instead of falling into fear like the disciples did, the Lord wants you to know He didn't cause the storm. If Jesus had thought that way, if He believed the Father had brought the storm for some greater good in His life, then He would have been going against the Father by rebuking the storm. So don't fall into that trap of believing everything that happens to you is God's will. In the world, you will have tribulation, but Jesus has overcome the world (John 16:33). It is not God's will for you to have trouble; it's for you to overcome the trouble and walk in continual triumph. It's the enemy who comes to steal, kill, and destroy. Jesus came to give you life in abundance.

So we have confidence that God has already declared His will for us to walk in triumph, and this judgment has already been declared in heaven and backed by His authority. We have access to it, and we can enforce it. When you get that bad diagnosis, for example, it comes up like a storm trying to derail you from your God-given purpose. Jesus and the disciples were headed toward a tremendous deliverance for a whole town, and the squall on the Sea of Galilee was trying to take them out. The disciples woke Jesus up and begged Him to do something. Jesus did not say any of the things we often say to ourselves: "I think we just need to bear it with godly character. If we drown, let's make sure we are a good example of sacrifice for others to follow." There would be a time for Jesus to sacrifice Himself, but this wasn't it. He knew it was not the Father's will for Him to perish on the sea. So based on that knowledge of God's will, He exercised His authority over the situation. "Peace, be still! Sea, be calm! Storm, stop!" Remember, Jesus didn't do these works on earth as God. He did them as a human being, showing us how we can do the works of God by faith. This was a demonstration of what we can do when the enemy starts blowing, growling, intimidating, and threatening to take us out. We can exercise our God-given authority in Jesus in exactly the same way, with confidence that we are walking in His will.

When you encounter adversity in your life, then do not fall into fear. Instead, pick up the sword of the Spirit, which is the Word of God. Put on His full armor (Ephesians 6:11–17). The breastplate of righteousness gives you confidence to know that whatever you ask for, you can receive. Your heart and your desires are protected by the righteousness of God. You never need to fear offering "illegal" prayers, as if you are intruding on territory you don't deserve. God has made you righteous, and even though you haven't earned the right to receive answers to your prayers, you have received righteousness by grace through faith. You've confessed your sin, He is faithful to forgive you and cleanse you of all your crookedness, and He is greater than any condemnation you feel in your heart. *"If our heart does not condemn us, we have confidence toward God. And whatever we ask we receive from Him" (1 John 3:21–22).* He has taken away your shame, cleared you of all accusations, and put you on a sure foundation. The breastplate of righteousness reminds you that you've been cleansed and have no business calling unclean what God has made clean.

Then pick up the shield of faith, which extinguishes every fiery dart. Put on the helmet of salvation and the shoes of the gospel of peace. You can go through every piece of armor and discover the power and protection God gives you to live and walk by faith. When the enemy comes with accusations, with adverse circumstances, with symptoms and diagnoses, you can pick up the shield of faith and say, "I'm not going to let that take root in my heart. I'm not going to buy into that lie. Storm, be still!" Then pick up the sword of the Spirit, which is the Word of God, and wield it with all the confidence that someone bearing the authority of Jesus should have.

Do not make the mistake of thinking that learning to speak life over yourself, other people, and your circumstances will make you immune to hardship.

There have been times when circumstances have been designed to completely take me out, situations that, if I had not believed I would see the goodness of the Lord in the land of the living, would have caused me to lose heart. I've had serious sickness come against me and the enemy coming at me in the middle of the night to say he was going to use it to kill me. I know what it is like to fear. I know what it's like to go through a hard time. Sometimes people have told me in these bleak situations that I must have caused them, that such bad things would not happen to me unless I had done something wrong or somehow opened a door to allow it in my life. I've had to resist the discouragements and temptations to get introspective and instead pick up the shield of faith and declare the truth: *"Many are the afflictions of the righteous, but the Lord delivers him out of them all (Psalm 34:19)*. Thank You, Lord, that You are my hope and my help. Thank You that You are the God who heals me and that by Your stripes I am healed." So even though I have felt intense fear at times, I have had the privilege of the Holy Spirit's encouragement to not give in to lies and human reasoning but to declare instead, "Thank You, God. I am the righteousness of God, and I am the healed of the Lord." I have found Him to be my ever-present help in times of trouble (Psalm 46:1). He reminds me of His Word, giving me just the right Scripture verse for the moment. He reveals the will of heaven. He makes His presence known. He encourages me and reminds me that I never need to be afraid or anxious about anything. He causes me to triumph continually.

This needs to become a foundation of our lives. If it is not, we will wobble when storms come. We will wonder what's going on, question why it is happening, and even accuse God for not preventing the hardship we are experiencing. I've learned in the midst of storms never to ask, "Why me, why this problem, why aren't You answering me?" It also doesn't help very much to ask why. The better question is, "Who are You, God? How do You want to reveal Yourself in this situation? You are my healer, my redeemer, my provider, my righteousness, my rescuer, my very present help in trouble. You are the glory and the lifter of my head." When we are going through adversity, we need to know, in the very core of our being, who He is.

You will never find yourself in a situation in which the Father is not right there with you, ready to release supernatural hope into your heart and remind you that He has already determined to give you triumph and lead you in victory. There isn't a single circumstance in your life in which the Lord has not already declared His will in heaven. When God is for you, who can be against you? It's time for you to reach up and say, "Thank You, Lord. I am coming into agreement with the Father, Son, and Holy Spirit. I'm saying yes, Your will be done on earth as it is in heaven. You have determined that I will walk in divine health. You have given me prosperity and abundance in all areas of life. With long life You will satisfy me and show me Your salvation." Then fill your mouth with words of victory. "Body, be healed. Flesh, be strengthened. Circumstances, obey the will of heaven. Storms, stop. Relationships, be restored." Speak out whatever the Holy Spirit has put into your heart. Just as Jesus spoke specifically to the storm, you can speak specifically to the situations in your life. Jesus did not say, "If it's Your will, Lord, do this for Me." He knew the Father and He knew the Father's will. He knew the storm threatening to kill Him was not the will of God. He told the wind and sea to be calm. You can do exactly the same thing in your life. Whatever the circumstances are with your spouse, your children, your health, your workplace, or wherever else, you can know God has promises for them. Those promises will lead you in triumph if you will declare them and stand firm in them by faith. All that is left for you to do is thank God that His Word will never return to Him void but will accomplish what He and what you sent it forth to do.

What circumstances are causing you to fear? What keeps you awake at night? What default thoughts are running in the background of your brain? It's easy for those thoughts to resurface at any time. Sometimes I think I'm doing pretty well, and then when I have some down time and relax a bit, some thought will come up and make me realize they've been ticking away in my brain the whole time. Those little nagging fears need to be exposed and then subjected to the sword of the Spirit. Declare the revealed will of God over them. Speak directly to the circumstances of your life and insist on the victory God has given you. Don't let those nagging thoughts steal your peace, even for a moment. God wants you to walk in supernatural peace through everything.

More and more, I am learning that God is more "for us" than any of us have ever realized. He is absolutely obsessed with our peace, our joy, our triumph. He is jealous to see us walk in the victory He has won for us. Like a newlywed husband who is vigilant over his new bride's every need, He is preoccupied with our happiness in Him. He is continually looking for ways to help us recognize that even though we have trouble in this world, He has overcome it. He does not want us to walk in discouragement, depression, fear, or anxiety. His kingdom is righteousness, peace, and joy in the Holy Spirit. He wants us to drink deeply from the river of His delight over us.

Remember, you are never a beggar trying to get His attention. He is already on your side. Jesus and the Holy Spirit are continually praying for you. The more you realize that, the more your heart is overwhelmed with awe, and the more your heart merges with His as one. You will love what He loves, hurt for what He hurts for, dream His dreams, and walk in His will. You will look into every situation that does not line up with His will and be able to speak life into it.

BIBLE VERSES ABOUT THE POWER OF WORDS

- A man will be satisfied with good by the fruit of his mouth (Proverbs 12:14).

- There is one who speaks like the piercings of a sword, but the tongue of the wise promotes health (Proverbs 12:18).

- The truthful lip shall be established forever, but a lying tongue is but for a moment (Proverbs 12:19).

- Lying lips are an abomination to the Lord, but those who deal truthfully are His delight (Proverbs 12:22).

- Anxiety in the heart of man causes depression, but a good word makes it glad (Proverbs 12:25).

- A soft answer turns away wrath, but a harsh word stirs up anger. The tongue of the wise uses knowledge rightly, but the mouth of fools pours forth foolishness (Proverbs 15:1–2).

- A wholesome tongue is a tree of life, but perverseness in it breaks the spirit (Proverbs 15:4).

- A man's stomach shall be satisfied from the fruit of his mouth; from the produce of his lips he shall be filled (Proverbs 18:20).

- Death and life are in the power of the tongue, and those who love it will eat its fruit (Proverbs 18:21).

- Whoever guards his mouth and tongue keeps his soul from troubles (Proverbs 21:23).

- A word fitly spoken is like apples of gold in settings of silver (Proverbs 25:11).

- Set a guard, O Lord, over my mouth; keep watch over the door of my lips (Psalm 141:3).

- "Assuredly, I say to you, whoever says to this mountain, 'Be removed and be cast into the sea,' and does not doubt in his heart, but believes that those things he says will be done, he will have whatever he says. Therefore I say to you, whatever things you ask when you pray, believe that you receive them, and you will have them" (Mark 11:23–24).

- Let no corrupt word proceed out of your mouth, but what is good for necessary edification, that it may impart grace to the hearers (Ephesians 4:29).

- Let your speech always be with grace, seasoned with salt, that you may know how you ought to answer each one (Colossians 4:6).

- Look also at ships: although they are so large and are driven by fierce winds, they are turned by a very small rudder wherever the pilot desires. Even so the tongue is a little member and boasts great things (James 3:4–5).

ABOUT THE
AUTHOR

Katherine Ruonala has a prophetic and healing ministry and travels internationally as a conference speaker bringing a message of love and hope to the nations. Katherine carries a strong prophetic and miracle anointing with many being instantly healed in her meetings. Reaching across denominational walls, her ministry is also used to spread the fires of revival and ignite a fresh passion in the hearts of believers to go deeper in their relationship with God. Katherine hosts her own television show *Katherine Ruonala TV* and is author of the best-selling books *Living in the Miraculous: How God's Love Is Expressed*

Through the Supernatural, Wilderness to Wonders: Embracing the Power of Process, and *Life with The Holy Spirit: Enjoying Intimacy with the Spirit of God*.

Katherine's husband, Tom Ruonala, is an accomplished business man and serves as the Honorary Consul of Finland in Brisbane. Katherine is the founder and coordinator of the Australian Prophetic Council and has appeared several times on Sid Roth's *It's Supernatural* television program, CBN, and other premium TV shows across the world. Katherine is also a Bible school graduate and a qualified music and high school teacher.

Katherine and Tom have been married for over twenty-eight years and have three beautiful children, Jessica, Emily, and Joseph.

CONTACT
KATHERINE RUONALA
MINISTRIES

Website: www.katherineruonala.com

Email: info@katherineruonala.com

**Write to us with your testimonies
or prayer requests**
Katherine Ruonala Ministries
PO Box 1077
Springwood, QLD 4123
Australia

INVITE KATHERINE TO SPEAK AT YOUR CHURCH OR EVENT

www.katherineruonala.com/invite-katherine/

VIEW OUR YOUTUBE CHANNEL FOR LIVE AND ARCHIVED SERVICES

www.youtube.com/glorygathering

Listen to the weekly podcast from Katherine Ruonala
and Glory City Church, available on iTunes.

**Help us spread the Good News by
partnering with us financially**

www.katherineruonala.com/donate

FIND US ON SOCIAL MEDIA:

Twitter: www.twitter.com/katherineruo
Instagram: www.instagram.com/katherineruonala
Facebook: www.fb.com/KatherineRuonalaMinistries

GLORY CITY CHURCH:

www.glorycitychurch.com.au

AUSTRALIAN PROPHETIC COUNCIL:

www.australianpropheticcouncil.com.au

OTHER BOOKS BY
KATHERINE
RUONALA

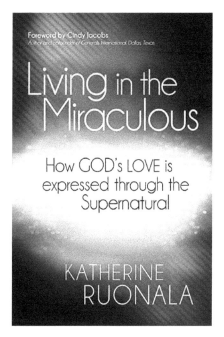

**You are fully, completely, and thoroughly adored
by God. And through His love you can live
a life full of miracles.**

Filled with inspirational personal stories and prophetic
revelations, *Living in the Miraculous* challenges you to
believe so completely in God's love for you that you expect
the miraculous in your life every day. Your faith flourishes
when you are rooted and grounded in God's love. When
you really see who He is and get a glimpse of His affection
for you, walking in His power becomes natural.

Are you praying for a loved one to be saved? Are you anticipating the fruition of a dream or desire?

In those times when you are waiting for the fulfillment of a promise, it is vital to seek understanding of God's divinely orchestrated purpose. *From Wilderness to Wonders* examines the journey—the one that takes believers through wilderness seasons full of tests and trials—and emphasizes the importance of enduring the process.

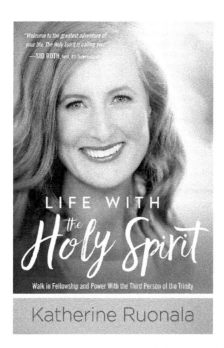

"Welcome to the greatest adventure of your life. The Holy Spirit is calling you!"
—SID ROTH, host, It's Supernatural!

LIFE WITH
the
Holy Spirit

Walk in Fellowship and Power With the Third Person of the Trinity

Katherine Ruonala

LIFE WITH THE HOLY SPIRIT

Fellowship with the Holy Spirit, encounter God in deeply personal ways, and release the power of the Holy Spirit in signs, wonders, and miracles.

Life with The Holy Spirit will discuss topics such as:

- How to see the fruit of the Spirit manifest in your life
- How to move in the gifts of the Holy Spirit
- The power of praying in the Spirit and the gift of tongues
- How to hear and see in the Spirit (visions, dreams, and revelation)
- How to partner with the Holy Spirit for healing and miracles

Lightning Source UK Ltd.
Milton Keynes UK
UKHW021158180919
350011UK00010B/1351/P

9 780648 556800